Second Edition

HELPING RESEARCHERS WRITE . . .

SO MANAGERS CAN UNDERSTAND

Second Edition

HELPING RESEARCHERS WRITE . . .

SO MANAGERS CAN UNDERSTAND

By Pneena Sageev

BATTELLE PRESS
Columbus • Richland

Printed in the United States of America.

Library of Congress Cataloging-in-Publication Data

Sageev, Pneena P.
    Helping researchers write—so managers can understand
    by Pneena Sageev. — 2nd ed.

    p.   cm.
    Includes bibliographical references (p. 168).
    ISBN 0-935470-77-8: $29.95

1. English language—Rhetoric. 2. English language—Technical English.
3. English language—Business English. 4. Business report writing.
5. Technical writing. I. Title.
PE1475.S25 1994
808' .0666—dc20   94-9994
                                                                    CIP

Battelle Press
505 King Avenue
Columbus, Ohio 43201-2693
614-424-6393
1-800-451-3543
Fax: 614-424-3819

CONTENTS

PREFACE TO THE FIRST EDITION

Is this book addressed to you? The answer is probably "Yes"—if you work in R&D as a scientist, engineer, manager, or director. If you're a technical editor, writing instructor, or student, you'll also likely benefit.

Here's why.

True, this book is aimed mainly at researchers in industry, or in R&D organizations such as Battelle, who need to write technical material to company managers. (We call such work "technical/business writing".) In fact, it's based on our survey and experience in this area.

But, as the book progressed, we realized that many of its suggestions also applied to:

■ Researchers in industry, universities, and other organizations working on projects funded by government agencies

■ University researchers, traditionally funded by government grants, who now are also actively seeking support from industry and other sources

■ Researchers working for the new R&D consortiums sponsored by several companies

■ Researchers working with the emerging R&D "Centers of Excellence" jointly established by companies, universities, state or federal agencies, or private foundations.

At the same time, the term "manager" took on a broader meaning. Again, the book primarily targets line or project managers and R&D executives working in industry. But here, too, we found that many ideas applied to decision makers and project monitors in other R&D-supporting organizations and agencies.

As the book evolved, we saw that **editors** can use it to broaden their role in helping researchers write better documents more efficiently. **Instructors**, too, can use this book to help pinpoint researchers' writing problems and to develop more effective, results-oriented, in-house writing courses.

Further, we saw an urgent need for universities to better prepare science and engineering students for writing tasks they will face in the "real world". Thus, **students** can use this book to find out what writing demands to expect from potential employers and how to respond. **University teachers** can also use it as a basis for building writing courses relevant to their students' future jobs.

In short, the book offers guidelines to researchers, managers, editors, instructors, and students on **CLIENT-ORIENTED TECHNICAL WRITING**. It suggests ways to write materials so that decision makers—who manage, monitor, or fund research—can more readily understand, and promptly apply, R&D results.

***

This book was not a single-handed effort. Dr. S.R. Simon, Manager of the Battelle Technical Inputs to Planning program (B-TIP), encouraged and supported the idea from the start. Yvonne Burry and Jack Mortland, senior editors for B-TIP publications, provided a constant sounding board, critiqued the early drafts, edited the book and wrote the "callouts"—the running summary in the margin. Dorothy Tonjes of ProWrite was our outside editor. Michah Sageev wrote the computer program for analyzing the responses to our questionnaire. Delphine Rucker, B-TIP's production assistant for publications, entered all the survey responses and generated the results. Brenda Switzer, our word processing operator, revised the later drafts. Dean Kette, the designer of B-TIP's publications, created the visuals to illustrate our ideas—and to add some fun. Battelle Press's Joe Sheldrick and Morrie Helitzer offered several useful suggestions. And of course, the reviewers—Richard Gudesen of Franklin International; Dr. Jay G. Otten of BASF Wyandotte Corporation; Dr. E. L. Rodriguez of Owens Corning Fiberglas; Dr. Robert Sherwood of FMC Corporation (formerly of Pennwalt Corporation); and Dr. Barney Cornaby, William Goldthwaite, and Dr. Robert Schwerzel of Battelle—all made extremely helpful suggestions and comments to improve the book's usefulness. Thanks also go to Dr. Richard Nathan, Dr. David Stahl, Dr. Michael Manahan, and Kathleen Moore of Battelle—a department manager, program manager, researcher, and editor at that time—who, through a series of interviews, explained how they successfully solved a difficult writing problem in their group.

But most of all, we have to thank the 1300 researchers and managers in industry and at Battelle who responded to our survey. Their input set the direction for this book.

Pneena Sageev
November 1986

PREFACE TO THE SECOND EDITION

Why publish a second edition of this book? ...So that you—the engineer, scientist, manager, director, educator, student, instructor, or editor—can benefit from two key developments that have emerged over the past seven years:

1. New experience, research results, and insights into teaching technical writing.

2. Radical advances in computer-based communication technologies.

To update you briefly, let's look at each factor in turn.

First, since 1987, we have been developing and teaching courses in technical communications—both written and oral—at the School of Engineering and Applied Sciences of the State University of New York at Buffalo. These courses, all based on the models and suggestions in this book, have encompassed various communication needs of both undergraduates and graduates. For example, the courses have ranged from

■ Semester-long classes that cover the main types of documents engineers and scientists write in the workplace, to

■ Shorter sessions on preparing written and oral reports that are integral to engineering laboratory and design courses, to

■ Graduate courses that focus on managing the written and oral communications work of engineering teams.

Further, seminars and workshops conducted in industry, government agencies, and universities have added new insights to our approach.

During this period, data from entrance and exit questionnaires have also provided concrete evidence of the writing problems engineers, scientists, and students perceive BEFORE the course—and the benefits they acquire AFTERWARDS.

All this experience and research clearly showed that the underlying writing problems revealed in our original survey remain largely the same.* The results also demonstrated the adaptability and effectiveness of our techniques, for example:

• The double-5 scheme for organizing content

• The editorial tools for creating shorter, simpler, and clearer sentences

• The basics of format for enhancing reading

• The efficiency methods for decreasing writing time.

Feedback from diverse course participants has been consistent: these problem-solving approaches and models really work!

Second, the rapid evolution of computerized communications has vastly changed the role of the computer for researchers' writing. It is now a "fact of life": computers are widely integrated into the workplace and universities. Though the exact extent of computer use for researchers' writing may not be documented**, our research—and common anecdotal evidence—show that such usage has grown enormously. The reasons are twofold: a) the vast increase in the capabilities and "user-friendliness" of word processing and desktop publishing since 1986; and b) the huge reductions in computer costs.

---

* Thus, Chapter 7 containing the detailed survey results has remained intact.

** See page 128 for more details on this issue.

Clearly, the computer has become a key player in reducing time to produce a document, or conversely, increasing researchers' capacity to produce more reports, proposals, or other written products within the same timeframe. It has also enabled researchers to markedly improve the quality and professional look of their written products.

Thus, in this revised edition, you will find:

- Additional materials on using the basic double-5 model for organizing content
- A fine-tuning of the editorial tools
- A complete revamp of the section on writing efficiently
- Updates on estimating costs and time for writing
- New suggestions to researchers, managers, and companies for applying our methods
- Realistic writing improvement rates researchers and managers can expect
- An updated "forecast" of trends—both business and technological—that will impact writing techniques.

Most important, useful examples from recent experience and research are peppered throughout this edition.

Now, let me thank those who encouraged and spurred the publication of this edition. Joe Sheldrick, the Publisher of Battelle Press, initiated the idea; then he firmly, yet kindly, kept it moving. Yvonne Burry, the present Publications Manager of the B-TIP program, provided excellent comments and suggestions throughout this project. Jack Mortland, B-TIP's Senior Editor, gave valuable suggestions on improving and simplifying the language(!). Yair Sageev, of "Icebreaker Information Processing & Consulting", keyed in and proofread the manuscript. He also suggested information for the computer-related sections, particularly on upcoming communications media and potential applications. The original art and cartoons were created by Dean Kette of "Design Communications". Gregg and Sara Klein of "In House Design Group" were responsible for the revised layout. Then, Rosalyn Gammerman, my colleague at the Engineering School at SUNY Buffalo, reviewed the final version.

But above all, I have to thank my entire family for their unfailing support...and patience.

Pneena Sageev
May 1994

Helping researchers write...

IN BRIEF

Of course researchers' written communication skills are important in industrial R&D! Companies realize that both new ideas and R&D results are not useful unless they are clearly reported to—and understood by—managers who decide on product development and future research investment.

But, despite this pivotal need, managers often have difficulty understanding what researchers write. And researchers, too, face serious problems in their writing tasks.

What exactly are these problems? And how can they be solved?

To answer these questions, in 1986, we surveyed researchers and managers in 150 companies worldwide to find out what main writing problems they face, what actions they take, and how effective these actions are. Then, we tapped our own nine years of experience working with researchers to publish technical information for managers.

The outcome: this book on "Helping Researchers Write ... So Managers Can Understand". The first six chapters

- Identify the main problems of researchers' technical/ business writing
- Suggest steps **researchers** can take
- Suggest steps **managers** can take
- Evaluate the potential results of these actions
- Recommend a group approach companies can use to establish writing improvement programs
- Present a scenario of trends in improving writing for industrial R&D use.

A seventh chapter, really an appendix, displays and discusses the numerical results of the 1986 survey.

Chapter I singles out the **main problems of researchers' technical/business writing** by analyzing the survey results and deriving conclusions. The results reveal, for example, that researchers and managers typically spend 20 to 40 percent of their time writing or reviewing technical/business documents—chiefly research reports, memos, and proposals. However, these documents often do not have the qualities both researchers and managers seek most: content that is clear, well organized, useful, logical, and concise. Further, despite the time dedicated to writing, researchers specified lack of time to complete documents properly as a major problem; many managers agreed. Though many researchers were eager to use them, computers were not widely used as a personal writing tool — 90 percent of researchers still primarily used pencil and paper. Researchers also had problems just starting a writing task.

The main problems managers reported with researchers' writing were difficulty in scanning and quickly grasping major points, poor organization, unclear logic, and lack of conclusions and recommendations. They also complained that researchers write long, awkward sentences that contain excessive jargon. Researchers, too, reported difficulty in constructing easy-to-read sentences and choosing the right words. Also, they had trouble selecting the information managers (or other requesters) need, identifying the right technical level for a document, clarifying the logic of conclusions, and organizing the information.

However, a vast gap emerged between **managers' perceptions** of the guidance, feedback, and other writing assistance they give, and **researchers' perceptions** of the help they receive. Managers claim they give much more help than researchers say they receive.

Such results lead us to conclude:

- Researcher's main writing problems lie in **content** (selecting and organizing relevant information), **strategies**[*] (using productive writing methods), and **style** (using language and format to create easy-to-read documents)—**in that order of priority.**
- The huge amount of time researchers and managers spend writing and reviewing, and the widely used inefficient writing procedures, reveal a severe productivity problem. In 1986, we estimated an annual writing-related cost to U.S. industry of $7 billion. In 1993, that number rose to $9.47 billion.
- The writing skills researchers need in an industrial R&D context are far more complex than those conventionally taught.
- Managers' help is **essential** to resolve these problems and upgrade researchers' skills—especially their productivity.
- However, many actions managers now take are not effective; they do not produce desired results.

Thus, this book focuses on three goals:

- Higher document quality—clear, useful, and logical information
- Greater writing productivity—more efficient and effective writing strategies
- Broader and better writing skills—that encompass both technical and business communications.

To meet these goals, the rest of the book is divided into two main thrusts: **solutions...and results**.

Chapter II covers **steps researchers can take**. It deals with the three main areas we've already delineated: how to improve **content, strategies,** and **style**. Under **content,** it deals with ways to select the right level of technical detail, and make sure this information is logical, complete, and concise. **Strategies** looks at suggestions to help researchers get started, write and edit a first draft, and solve time-crunch problems. The section on **style** uses real examples to point out common errors...and suggests ways to correct them.

But fundamental to all our practical suggestions is a method for organizing reports, memos, proposals, and other technical/business documents that helps bridge the communications gap between researchers and managers. Our method draws on science's 5-part problem solving approach — Problem, Apparatus, Method, Observations, Conclusions—but tailors it to business as well as technical needs. We call it the "double-5 organizational scheme". It also forms the basis for selecting needed technical and business information and assuring logic, completeness, and clarity. It even underlies more efficient methods to outline documents and schedule their preparation. We recommend that both researchers and managers use it.

---

* To reflect a broader approach, the word "strategies" in this edition replaces the original term, "procedures".

Helping researchers write...

However, researchers cannot apply all these actions alone: they must have managers' active support. Thus, Chapter III suggests **steps managers can take.** It's divided into two sections:

- **Immediate steps** that can be implemented directly by managers, without additional costs—but with changes in task, attitude, and time allocation. Such steps include, for example, establishing clear guidelines for preparing documents, checking outlines **before** writing begins, and giving constructive feedback on **content**—without editing. These steps, too, can be based on the double-5 organizational scheme.

- **Long-term steps** that require substantial funding—but that yield far greater improvements in writing quality, productivity, and skills. For example, making computers easily accessible to increase writing productivity, streamlining writing requirements to reduce writing time, initiating work-based in-house writing courses designed to solve specific problems, and hiring professional editors to rapidly upgrade document quality. To illustrate how an editor can be effectively used, we include an example from an R&D department.

But, suppose you do implement our suggestions. **What results can you expect?** That's what Chapter IV discusses. Then, in a summary chart, it compares the impacts of these steps on our three writing improvement goals (better quality, productivity, and language skills); expected rates of improvement; and relative costs and time for implementation.

Broadly, we believe that actions to upgrade content—primarily through a unified organizational approach—will yield the greatest gains in document quality, but will also improve writing skills and productivity. The primary benefits of improved writing strategies—better outlining, use of computers, editorial help, better time management—can yield enormous productivity gains, but will also benefit document quality. Improvements in style—better sentence structure and word choice, avoidance of jargon, and use of format to enhance understanding—are apt to be gradual. However, rates of improvement will vary with researchers' talent, experience, and adaptability, and with managers' support and encouragement.

So, with continuing effort, researchers and managers who apply these steps can reasonably expect:

- Incremental improvements in researchers' language skills, not magic conversions to slick copy

- Significant savings in researchers' time to write and managers' time to read or review

- Substantial—even dramatic—improvements in document content and quality.

Chapter V looks at all these suggested steps from an **organization** or **company view**. It particularly addresses top management whose sustained support—and even enthusiasm—is essential for success. It then describes a stepwise process an R&D group of **any** size could use to develop and implement a Writing Improvement Program. The program plan, based on a "writing audit", determines the group's specific writing problems, defines objectives for our three writing goals, and specifies solutions and implementation details.

However, companies initiating such a program should expect long-term, steadily increasing returns on investment, not instant payoffs.

From a still broader industrial R&D perspective, Chapter VI "forecasts" **future trends in improving researchers' technical/business writing**. It also discusses the incentives and roadblocks to the growth of these trends. In this edition, we revaluate this "forecast".

In our view, two main problems will spur many companies to take action, even urgent action:

- The high cost in time and money consumed by writing and reading technical/business documents
- The inadequate quality and timeliness of these documents.

Therefore, we expect many companies to take several steps recommended here—such as providing researchers with their own computers, hiring technical editors, adopting a basic organizational scheme for their technical/business documents, and streamlining writing requirements.

However, to attack the problem closer to the root, we anticipate companies encouraging universities to develop or bolster mandatory technical/business writing courses, and even to introduce courses in technical/business editing. But, for more immediate solutions, we anticipate growth of custom-designed in-house courses.

As a result of these trends, we foresee far reaching changes in the ways both researchers and managers go about their writing-related tasks. Though these changes are apt to occur gradually, the bottom line will show a tangible reduction in time spent writing and reading researchers' documents, yet a vast gain in quality. Our estimate: a 5 percent reduction in total writing time is readily attainable; a 10 percent reduction is often feasible; and up to a 45 percent reduction is sometimes possible.

And the ultimate impact? If:

- Researchers seriously undertake actions to upgrade their writing skills and products,
- Managers actively provide the sustained help, tools, and support for researchers to improve their writing, and
- Managers and researchers remember that the road to improvement is long and arduous,

then:

researchers will more productively write higher quality documents...
that managers will understand better and use more effectively.

HELPING RESEARCHERS WRITE

. . . SO MANAGERS CAN UNDERSTAND

CHAPTER I

MAIN PROBLEMS
IN RESEARCHERS'
TECHNICAL/BUSINESS WRITING

MAIN PROBLEMS IN RESEARCHERS' TECHNICAL/BUSINESS WRITING

• Need for technical/business writing skills • Problem: Identifying main writing deficiencies
• Solution: Conduct a survey • Highlights of survey results • Conclusions...and focus for this book

---

The need for technical/business writing skills

You only have to look at the advertisements for scientists and engineers—whether in the Wall Street Journal or in your company's internal newsletter—to realize how important researchers' writing skills are. For example, the ads tell us:

How important are good writing skills for researchers?

...quid and ...or fractured media and transport of dissolved or colloidal materials. Excellent verbal and written communication skills are required. Experience in waste disposal processes is desirable. (BPMD 286-031)

...sion engineer. ON...

Microbiologi...
Job responsibilities include:
• Develop strategy and plans for project work
• Supervise fermentation project work and personnel
• Coordinate all in-house and outside company project activities

Good written/oral communication skills are essential. Prefer M.S. or Ph.D. or 4-6 years equivalent experience i... Microbial Ph... ...mistry. 2-3...

...ssful candidate... degree in Toxicology, Pathology...Sciences, and will probably have additional qualifications in Veterinary Sciences. The candidate will already have experience with the toxicology of pharmaceuticals, have an established reputation through publications, have knowledge of the international requirements of drug regulatory agencies, and be prepared to meet with these agencies when required, will have excellent written and oral communication skills and will interact closely with, and travel frequently to the re...ch laboratories in...

Applicants should have:
• expertise in the isolation a... ...aff (glyco) proteins. Familiarity with r... desirable but not essential.
• a Ph.D. in Biochemistry.
• 0 - 3 years postdoctoral experience.
• a growing publication record.
• clear and concise communication skills.

...W offer excellent compensation and b...

...echnology and knowledge of relevant manufacturing processes. Must have excellent writing and oral communication skills and the ability to fulfill major market development assignments in the industrial and government sectors. Should be abl... ...n and manage research p...

...th care products. Due to our continued ...newly created opportunity available for ...h a strong interest and experience in documentation... ...paration, to join our Clinical Research Operations Group...

Qualified candidates should have a Ph.D. in Pharmacology or Microbiology or equivalent with a minimum of 5 years experience in basic research, scientific documentation and computer application. Excellent writing skills are essential. You will be responsible for analyzing, integrating and supervising the preparation of documents from information gathered primarily from the Clinical Research area. These documents will be utilized in support of New Drug Applications and related scientific publications. Additional responsibilities include document plan... ...gn, manual ...dination of

...qualify, you must have a BSEE or BSME, and four years' ...erience in airborne military/commercial turbine engine electrical ...mponent design and development. You must also have some ...rect experience in aerospace packaging methods and materials processes, and the environments associated with these products. Effective oral and written communications skills are essential, and a background in technical liaison with customers will be considered helpful.

You should have a Ph.D. degree... ...netics, biochemistry... related life science, preferably with three to six years of experience after the Ph.D. A strong background in basic science and solid laboratory experience in gene mutation, cytogenetics and/or DNA damage assays are essential, as are superior oral and written communications skills.

...ffer... xcellent salary and bene...ts progr... including

Look at the qualifications employers seek,

▶

..."excellent written and verbal communication skills required"... ..."demonstrated ability to prepare successful proposals and write technical reports"... "evidence of advanced communication skills, both written and oral, must be provided"... "must have excellent communication skills, written and verbal"...

In the survey we conducted to provide the basis for this book, one manager emphasized this need. He wrote:

and the attitudes R&D managers express.

▶

"I believe that there is a strong correlation between the writing skills and the research skills of an individual...that writings are a strong indicator of the level of understanding an individual has of the subject matter, and of the diligence the individual takes in his or her research."

Another even went on to say:

"We need to impress on researchers that how they communicate is probably more important than what they actually do in the lab or the pilot plant."

Problem: Identifying main writing deficiencies

But exactly why researchers' writing is often hard for managers to understand is not clear.

However, while the need for such writing capabilities is widely recognized, the problems that researchers have in writing technical/business documents—

and that managers have in understanding this material—have not been so clearly identified.

Helping researchers write...

During B-TIP's[*] first nine years, the author and publication staff worked closely with researchers to clearly report technical and business information that is both useful and understandable to managers. Feedback from B-TIP members indicated that the end product usually attained its goal: it was useful and "well written".

During this time, as we identified major writing problems, we also developed solutions that improved quality and reduced time requirements both for researchers and editors.

Thus, we decided to share our findings. Our goal: to help alleviate writing problems—make it easier for researchers to write and for managers to read what researchers write. Our intent: to offer practical suggestions based on our experience.

Indeed, when the subject, "Helping Scientists Write...So Managers Can Understand" was placed on the list of potential topics for B-TIP publications, it received resounding approval from members.[**] Clearly, we had touched a sensitive nerve.

After working closely with researchers for 9 years, B-TIPS's publication staff pinpointed some major writing problems...

and found practical solutions to help upgrade researchers' writing and speed managers' comprehension.

Solution: Conduct a survey

To identify more precisely the technical/business writing problems in industry, we surveyed researchers and managers, both in B-TIP member companies and at Battelle. We hoped to learn:

■ What are the main writing problems that plague researchers?

■ What are the main difficulties managers face in reading and using researchers' written material?

To help develop practical solutions, we also wanted to know:

■ What kinds of documents do researchers need to write—and managers read?

■ How much time is devoted to this writing and reading?

■ What qualities should such writing have?

■ What efforts are researchers and managers making—or willing to make—to alleviate the problems they pinpointed?

■ How successful have some of these efforts been?

The size of the response amazed us: 1307 replies arrived from 70 companies worldwide and from Battelle. But even more encouraging than these numbers were the pertinent comments that respondents added. Now we had a solid basis for proceeding.

Further, we broadly surveyed researchers and managers to improve our understanding and knowledge of:

Replies, including many helpful comments and suggestions, came from more than 1300 managers and researchers in companies worldwide.

[*] Started in 1977, B-TIP (Battelle Technical Inputs to Planning) is a subscription program that informs industry's executives and managers about emerging technologies—their practical applications, business implications, and opportunities. Program members represent a cross-section of major corporations worldwide.

[**] Survey of "Potential Topics for B-TIP Publication", conducted November 1982.

Highlights of survey results

The results, fully summarized in the final chapter (page 139) are highlighted here.

The numerical results of the survey are summarized and discussed in the last chapter, starting on page 139. Many of you may find them interesting and useful. Here we'll highlight the results that set the direction for this book.

■ Reports, proposals, and memos are the main documents researchers write and managers read.

Overall, researchers and managers spend 20 to 40 percent of their time working with reports, proposals, and memos.

■ Typically, researchers and managers spend 20 to 40 percent of their time writing or reading these documents! Some spend even more time.

They expect these qualities:

■ The main qualities managers and researchers want in these technical/business documents are:

▶
  • Clarity
  • Easy-to-read technical explanations
  • Conciseness
  • Logical, readily grasped organization
  • Relevant information.

Such documents help companies:

■ Companies use these written materials mainly to:

▶
  • Communicate R&D results throughout the company
  • Decide on R&D directions and investments
  • Identify and evaluate new product concepts

and also, as respondents commented, to:

  • Keep tabs on research progress
  • Avoid "reinventing the wheel" or duplicating efforts.

But managers have problems with researchers' writing:

■ The main problems **managers** identify in researchers' writing are:

▶
  • Information is hard to scan and grasp quickly
  • Organization is poor or cumbersome
  • Logic leading to conclusions is unclear
  • Conclusions and recommendations are not spelled out
  • Sentences are poorly constructed
  • Too much jargon is used
  • Word choice is imprecise
  • Document focus is unclear
  • Documents are too long.

Several managers noted that research is often written up late—a major problem.

and researchers, too, have difficulties:

■ The main writing problems **researchers** face are:

▶
  • Deciding what level of technical information to include
  • Making sure the logic leading to conclusions is clear
  • Organizing the document to boost comprehension

- Figuring out what information the manager really wants to know
- Structuring easy-to-read sentences
- Choosing exact words
- Finding large enough chunks of time to write efficiently
- Getting started
- Writing the first draft
- Producing quality writing within allotted budgets.

■ Both researchers and managers ranked problems in grammar, spelling, punctuation, and format as the least important.

■ In 1986, despite the "advent" of the computer age, 90 percent of researchers still used pencil and paper as their main writing tools.[*]

The computer age? In 1986 pen and paper were still the main writing tools for 90 percent of researchers.[*]

■ As groups, managers and researchers do not agree on how much help is available to facilitate writing.

Managers and researchers disagree on the amount of help available for writing tasks...

■ Similarly, managers' and researchers' opinions differ widely on the kind and amount of guidance and feedback they give and receive. For example, about 40 percent of managers say they give researchers a general outline of documents; only 14 percent of researchers say they receive such outlines. The detailed results on pages 152 and 153 clearly delineate this gap in perception.

the amount of guidance given, and...

■ Researchers say their writing would improve most if they had their own computers and more time to do a better job. Managers, on the other hand, are most willing to fund writing courses and do performance reviews on improvements in writing skills. Few indicate they would add equipment. (See footnote.)

the best ways to facilitate writing.

■ Most of the respondents note that improving their ease of writing or reading technical/business materials would be "very" or "extremely" helpful. Only 2.5 percent said it would not be helpful. Such results clearly demonstrate the need and willingness to upgrade writing skills and products.

But they agree that steps to make writing easier would be useful.

■ About 55 percent of managers note that courses are offered to upgrade researchers' writing skills; but only about 20 percent of researchers say such help is available.

■ The majority of managers are willing to send researchers to in-house writing courses.

■ However, the effects of courses researchers already attended are discouraging: only about 26 percent of researchers noted specific improvements; only 13 percent of managers saw lasting improvements.

While managers are willing to support writing courses, gains from past instruction have not been encouraging.

■ Researchers give themselves higher marks for their writing than managers give them.

In view of these replies, what conclusions can we draw?

Thus...

---

[*] By 1994, this situation has probably changed in many companies. Overall computer availability has increased; computer use has expanded—sometimes dramatically.

Conclusions . . . and focus for this book

The survey results solidly defined the main problems that researchers face in writing technical/business documents—and that managers face in reading these materials. The results also shed light on other key issues: the most important qualities of technical/business documents, steps now taken to facilitate writing, and steps needed to help researchers upgrade their writing.

Survey results defined problems and highlighted key issues.

This information, together with our experience, led us to several conclusions.

We concluded:

1 For the main technical/business documents they need to write and read—reports, proposals, and memos—researchers and managers spelled out the meaning of "quality": clear, logical, concise and useful information.

For both researchers and managers, "quality" means clear, logical, concise, and useful information—an emphasis on content.

Note that these qualities all relate to **content**; in fact, the main purpose of such documents is to communicate research results or plans to other members of the organization. Managers and researchers both stress the importance of logic; managers particularly emphasize the need for logical conclusions, so they can use the information to decide on future business strategies, determine R&D directions, and prevent duplication of effort. They also want information to be clear and easy to scan so they can grasp what they need more rapidly.

Thus, to help upgrade document quality, this book must focus on ways to improve content.

2 Content also turned out to be the most fundamental writing problem for researchers. While managers have difficulty understanding what researchers write, or grasping a clear message, researchers have problems figuring out what managers really want to know. Researchers struggle particularly with decisions on how much technical detail to include.

But researchers have their own problems with content: What information do managers really want? In what detail?

Here again, we concluded that suggestions to resolve these content-related questions deserve top priority.

 However, the results also revealed an enormous writing **productivity** problem. Examine the next chart closely.

Productivity is a major problem.

These results lead to some crucial questions about R&D cost benefits and productivity:

- Are R&D organizations aware that such large amounts of time are spent on written communications?
- Are such expenditures of time justified?
- Are researchers properly equipped and trained for such writing tasks?
- If not, how does this deficiency impact the cost benefits R&D organizations obtain from their staffs?
- What steps can R&D organizations take—can researchers and managers take—to increase the ratio of research-to-writing time, yet upgrade the quality of researchers' writing?

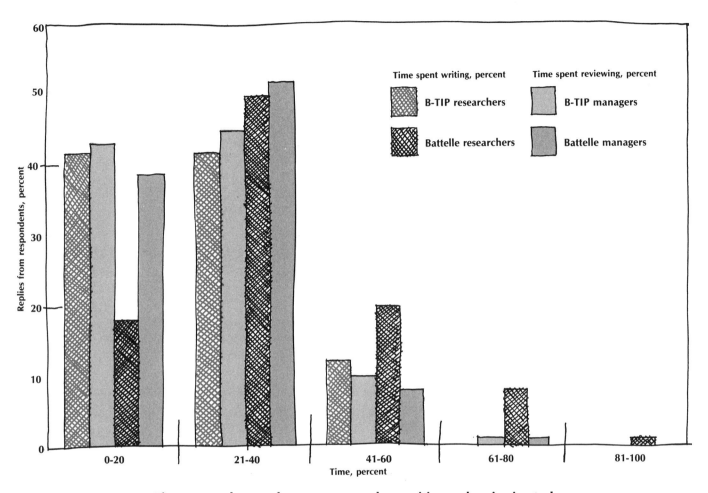

Time researchers and managers spend on writing and reviewing tasks

Indeed, the survey results carry a sobering message to industry: typically, between 20 and 40 percent of researchers' and R&D managers' time is spent writing and reading about research. For convenience, let's conservatively average that figure to 28 percent.*

Researchers and managers spend about 28 percent of their time writing and reading technical/business documents...

To appreciate the size of this productivity problem, let's look at some numbers. According to Battelle's estimate, in 1993 U.S industry will spend $83 billion on its own research and will perform a total of $112.7 billion of research.[2] Suppose we estimate conservatively that 30 percent of that expenditure will go to cover researchers' and line R&D managers' salaries (**not** including R&D directors or executives). Then, using our 28 percent figure for average writing or reading time, we arrive at the high annual cost for writing and reading technical/business documents of $6.98 billion (based on the $83 billion expenditure) or $9.47 billion (based on the $112.7 billion expenditure)! Readers can try estimating their companies' costs and extrapolating what savings a 5 percent productivity improvement would yield.

at an annual cost to U.S. industry of $9.47 billion!

* In fact, if we take into account the well documented tendency to underestimate the amount of time spent on a task, that figure could actually be much higher. Note that a detailed study for one company's R&D division, conducted by MIT, concluded that an average of 35 percent of researchers' and their supervisors' time was spent on writing-related tasks. See reference 1.

Thus, this book emphasizes more efficient writing strategies.

Problems in "language mechanics" center on style—sentence structure, word choice, and jargon;

spelling, grammar, and punctuation are much less important.

Managers as a group need more know-how to help researchers, and more effective ways to expedite writing.

Yet, many researchers maintained (and managers admitted) that they write under enormous time and budget constraints. They do not have sufficient uninterrupted time or quiet to write quality documents.

Thus, the importance of increasing writing productivity takes on a new perspective and urgency. This problem mandated that we suggest alternative, more efficient writing **strategies**.

4 The main problems in "mechanics" centered on the stylistic components: simplifying sentence structure, improving word choice, and decreasing use of jargon. We therefore decided to deal mainly with these three elements and to call that area "**style**".

5 From the survey results, we concluded that problems in **content, strategies,** and **style** (as defined above) are far more important than those in the strictly mechanical areas of spelling, grammar, and punctuation.

6 The help that managers provide may need to be reoriented. Managers' and researchers' extremely diverse perception of this assistance can lead to several possible conclusions:

◼ Managers are trying to facilitate researchers' writing; but their help is not effective—e.g., the kinds of courses, general outlines, and editorial assistance they offer are not yielding the desired results.

◼ Managers are not giving researchers clear guidelines and feedback. For example, about 47 percent of managers say they give researchers feedback on both basic and specific writing problems. Only 14 percent of researchers agree.

■ Many managers are not taking relatively easy, helpful steps such as telling researchers how long a document should be. This simple guideline could immediately help researchers determine the level of technical information they can cover.

■ Some managers may deliberately "not interfere" in researchers' writing.[*] This approach emerges not only from the numerical results but from several managers' comments.

In short, some managers may not know **how to help** researchers.

Still, many managers recognize the problems researchers face and indicate a willingness to help. Researchers, too, are eager to upgrade their writing. Since strong managerial support can be crucial to resolving writing problems, we look closely at this area and suggest more effective steps managers can take.

7 Our overall conclusion from the results: researchers' writing problems are far more complex than we may have realized. Often, "writing skills" are viewed simplistically as use of good sentence and paragraph structure, proper grammar, and correct punctuation and spelling.

Finally, researchers face complex writing problems that go beyond conventional writing skills.

However, **in an industrial R&D context, the key writing skills lie in selecting the most relevant, useful technical/business information, and organizing it clearly and logically to help readers understand the main points quickly.** No adroitness with sentence structure can compensate for useless information. Further, strategies for writing can strongly impact researchers' productivity and their documents' quality.

Note that

Thus, any actions we suggest... and that researchers and managers undertake... should be evaluated in light of their contribution to **three writing goals:**

So, solutions should be geared to obtaining:

■ **Higher document quality**—to meet our definition of quality: clear, logical, concise, and useful information

■ **Greater writing productivity**—to produce quality documents more quickly

■ **Broader and better language skills**—to enable managers (or other clients) to understand and use the information readily.

The rest of this book focuses on actions to help achieve these goals. It is divided into the following chapters:

...goals we focus on here.

Steps researchers can take

Steps managers can take

Results to expect

Developing writing improvement programs for R&D organizations

Outlook: Trends in improving researchers' technical/business writing

---

[*] In fact, 6 percent of managers say they give **no** guidance. (But 35 percent of researchers say they receive no guidance!)

But remember that

this book tries to meet the needs for improved, client-oriented writing of both English and non-English speakers.

Though it cannot be a "cure all", it does offer practical steps to upgrade researchers' writing...

to meet managers' needs.

But before we dig in, please remember a few caveats:

■ Even though English has become the most widely used language for discussing technology, this book is not aimed specifically at English-speaking writers or readers. On the contrary: responses from companies worldwide showed that writing problems are endemic to technology/business communications, not to any particular language. As much as possible, we have tried to structure the solutions to meet these international, multilingual needs. Thus, suggestions for improving content are broadly applicable; those on style, only partially apply to other languages. However, productivity suggestions are intended for **all** writers and readers of R&D communications.

■ "Soft areas" such as tone and "persuasiveness", often related to a specific culture, are not covered here *per se*. However our whole thrust is aimed at **client-oriented** writing—writing that addresses the clients' needs and enables client/readers to readily absorb and use the information it contains. Such writing is fundamental to persuasiveness in any setting.

■ Of course, we can't provide cures to all researchers' technical/business writing ills! But we can—and do—offer a unified, flexible system for identifying and organizing relevant content. This approach forms the basis for clearly communicating technical information to managers. We also offer tested solutions for dealing with many other real-life writing problems. Our main hope is that researchers and managers will find this book **useful**; that it will be a genuine starting point for improving writing quality, skills, and productivity.

But now, let's start discussing solutions—practical steps you can take.

CHAPTER II

STEPS RESEARCHERS CAN TAKE

STEPS RESEARCHERS CAN TAKE

This chapter covers steps researchers can take in three main areas:
● Content ● Strategies for writing ● Style: Language and format

Content

In suggesting steps researchers can take to improve content, we aim to help them overcome some of the writing problems they identified, and produce documents that have the key desirable qualities all survey respondents wanted. We cover:

To help researchers improve content, we discuss:

■ Organizing a technical/business document

■ Deciding on—and writing at—the right level of technical detail

■ Making documents more concise—and shorter

■ Attaining clarity

■ Facilitating reading and grasp

■ Achieving focus, completeness, and logic.

Organizing a technical/business document

In this section, we explain why good organization is crucial to efficiently producing quality documents, suggest an organizational scheme, show how it works, and apply the scheme to the main types of documents researchers write.

Why the emphasis on organization?

Both researchers and managers agree that good organization is a key ingredient of a well-written technical/business document. But it is also the key to resolving many writing problems for researchers and reading difficulties for managers. Consider that:

■ Organization provides the framework on which to hang ideas; it forms the basis for presenting thoughts in a **logical, coherent sequence that is readily understood by the reader.**

Good organization of documents can improve coherence, guide information selection, and stimulate innovation.

■ A sound, practical organizational scheme can also help researchers decide on the **content** of the document; it can guide them in **selecting and developing specific information** for each section of the document. It also helps them produce a useful, concise, yet complete, document.

■ At the same time, a good framework is not confining; rather, it can **stimulate ideas** and suggest how to place them in a readily grasped order.

To develop a useful organizational scheme, let's first look at the typical features of researchers' writing and the needs of business managers (see table on page 18).

Typical features of researchers' journal writing and managers' R&D communication needs

Feature	Researchers' writing for technical journals	Managers' R&D communications needs
Emphasis	Content	Content
Purpose	To convey research progress on a problem	To help resolve a problem or issue, or to exploit a technology opportunity
Audience	Other scientists in the field	R&D or other managers; many are trained in science, but are not specialists in areas they must read about
Level of technical detail	Often highly detailed	Usually less detailed
Technical terms	Because of peer audience, technical terms and jargon are not always problematical[*]	Jargon is a serious obstacle to understanding
Length	Varies; depends on journal	Concise, short documents
Readability	Not always specified; often hard to read[*]	Clear, unambiguous writing that is easy to read and scan
Information needs	Strictly technical	Technical **and** related business information
Use	To disseminate scientific information for evaluation and as a basis for further research	Scientific information is basis for business decisions on future products and R&D
Organization	Typical scientific, problem-solving, reporting scheme	More flexible; but must also contain action-oriented conclusions and recommendations

[*] But some journals' guidelines (e.g., of the American Chemical Society) urge authors to write more clearly and to minimize the use of jargon. See reference 3.

A suggested organizational scheme

To accommodate the requirements of both researchers and managers, we need a generic—yet flexible—organizational technique that is based on a problem-solving approach. Here's why.

Document organization should follow a problem-solving approach, already familiar to researchers,

Research projects always aim to resolve problems; so all documents surrounding that effort can, and should, be organized according to **scientific problem-solving principles**. This approach is convenient for researchers; in fact, it's an inherent outgrowth of their training.

For research managers, it's also a convenient, efficient, no-frills approach. However, while researchers may be prepared to spend time deciphering a difficult technical article, managers want to learn about research progress as quickly and painlessly as possible. Managers also need to know the business implications of research. For example:

that includes information managers need:

- When will a project be finished?
- Are the actual results as good as originally anticipated?

- Is the project on schedule, or are there unexpected bottlenecks and difficulties? ◀

- If difficulties are appearing, what do they mean? Are they surmountable? If so, how can they be overcome? Is the effort worthwhile?

- How soon can the results be turned into a marketable product?

- Will a patent position result?

- What are the new technology's business implications for the company? What are its advantages and disadvantages? Will it offer new opportunities? Or will it be a threat to current products? From a feasibility view, are manufacturing, environmental, and safety issues addressed? What implementation costs and return on investment are projected?

- How are the competitors reacting?

- What beneficial steps can the company take?

To meet the needs of both researchers and managers, we suggest an organizational technique for technical/business writing that has proved very effective in our publication work. We call it the **double-5 organizational scheme**. The technique uses science's problem-solving structure for conveying technical information; but it adds a parallel structure for interpreting technical information in business terms. We believe that, properly used, this framework can be the single most important factor in helping researchers improve the overall quality of their written output.

We suggest a five-part organizational scheme that translates basic steps of the scientific method into business terms.

How it works

Our double-5 organizational scheme starts with the standard scientific method for conducting and recording experiments:

- Define objective
- Select apparatus
- Determine method
- Make observations
- Draw conclusions.

We can change the particular terms to suit a technical/business environment, but the basic logical thought process remains the same. This principle is the key to using such a system for communications between researchers and managers.

For use in a business setting, the steps in the scientific method translate into the following terms:

We call this scheme "double-5" because it covers these five key terms from both technical and business views:

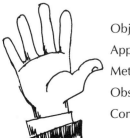

Objective	Problem
Apparatus	Scope
Method	Solution
Observations	Results
Conclusions	Conclusions

"DOUBLE-5": A GENERIC ORGANIZATIONAL SCHEME FOR TECHNICAL/BUSINESS DOCUMENTS

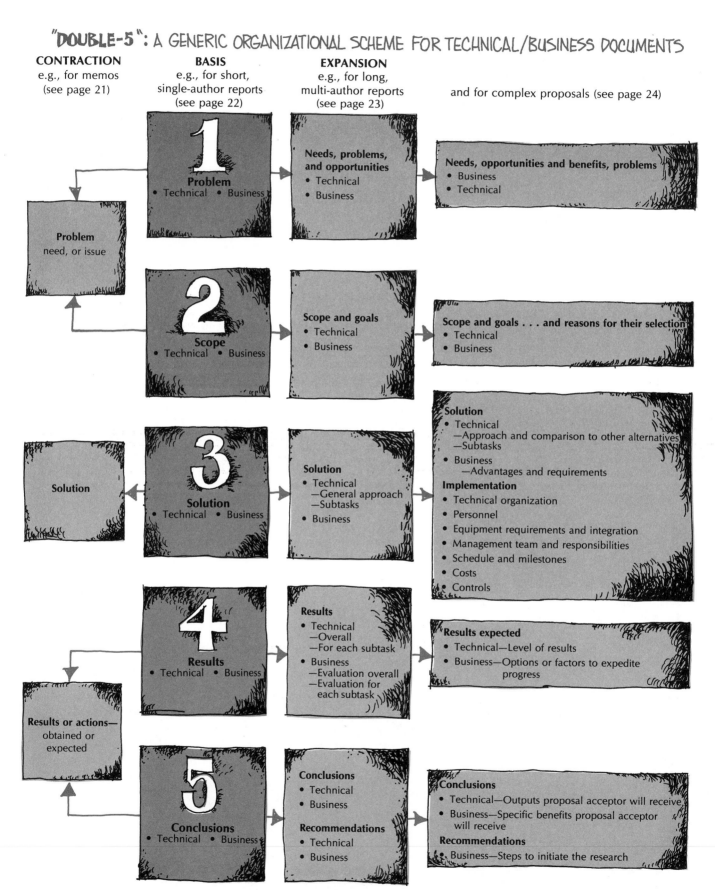

CONTRACTION
e.g., for memos
(see page 21)

BASIS
e.g., for short,
single-author reports
(see page 22)

EXPANSION
e.g., for long,
multi-author reports
(see page 23)

and for complex proposals (see page 24)

1 Problem
• Technical • Business

Needs, problems,
and opportunities
• Technical
• Business

Needs, opportunities and benefits, problems
• Business
• Technical

Problem
need, or issue

2 Scope
• Technical • Business

Scope and goals
• Technical
• Business

Scope and goals . . . and reasons for their selection
• Technical
• Business

3 Solution
• Technical • Business

Solution
• Technical
—General approach
—Subtasks
• Business

Solution

Solution
• Technical
—Approach and comparison to other alternatives
—Subtasks
• Business
—Advantages and requirements

Implementation
• Technical organization
• Personnel
• Equipment requirements and integration
• Management team and responsibilities
• Schedule and milestones
• Costs
• Controls

4 Results
• Technical • Business

Results
• Technical
—Overall
—For each subtask
• Business
—Evaluation overall
—Evaluation for
each subtask

Results expected
• Technical—Level of results
• Business—Options or factors to expedite
progress

Results or actions—
obtained or
expected

5 Conclusions
• Technical • Business

Conclusions
• Technical
• Business

Recommendations
• Technical
• Business

Conclusions
• Technical—Outputs proposal acceptor will receive
• Business—Specific benefits proposal acceptor
will receive

Recommendations
• Business—Steps to initiate the research

To incorporate managers' needs into this framework, we address each part of the organizational scheme from both technical and business viewpoints.

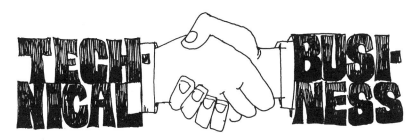

How it can be applied to different kinds of documents*

The double-5 scheme is especially useful because it applies to the types of technical/business documents researchers write most...from short memos or progress reports, to single-task research reports, to large multi-authored and multi-task research reports, to complex proposals. (See table on page 20.) Here's how it can be used.*

A key advantage is its adaptability to memos, reports, and proposals—the main documents researchers write.

Memo or business letter

For a memo or business letter, we would simplify the scheme by **contracting** it. Thus, our pattern for writing a memo would be:

For a memo, the organizational scheme is abbreviated to:

■ Problem, need, or issue

■ Solution

■ Results expected or actions to be taken.

Let's look at each of these elements more closely.

Problem, need, or issue	Clearly, memo writers, whether researchers or managers, have a problem or issue they want resolved. For example: managers may want researchers to submit progress reports earlier; researchers may urgently need a new piece of equipment.
Solution	Memo writers should always suggest a solution. For example: the managers may suggest writing short, 1-page progress reports that can easily be produced on time. Researchers may suggest ordering the new piece of equipment at "the best available price" ($—-) from ABC company, and funding the purchase from the AA (Advanced Automation) project.
Expected results or actions	Memo writers must clearly state the actions they expect. For example: the managers expect the 1-page summaries to start flowing in by the end of this month. The researchers need quick approval because it takes 6 weeks for the equipment to arrive. Alternatively, memo writers must state the actions they have already taken to resolve the problem or meet the need.

* Although we're addressing researchers' writing problems, managers can also use these ideas for writing their reports!

Research project report

To write a research project report on a single task—let's say, on work to resolve a specific production problem—researchers would directly use all parts of the double-5 scheme.

A single-task research report uses all five elements "as is"...

For example, suppose researchers were asked to solve a specific problem that was plaguing production of a primary product. Here's how the report framework might look:

Problem	**Technical:** To resolve the machining problem on the gear housing production line.
	Business: The business impacts of this problem were:
	■ 20 percent rejection rate
	■ Late deliveries
	■ Potential for rapid market share reduction.
Scope	**Technical:** What technical factor had to be addressed to resolve this problem?
	Business:
	■ Why was that also the key factor from a business view?
	■ What business goals or constraints applied?
Solution	**Technical:**
	■ What approach was taken to resolve the problem?
	■ What specific tasks were performed?
	Business:
	■ What business-related tasks or analyses were conducted?
	■ Did the research proceed as planned or were there unexpected difficulties?
	■ How were these difficulties resolved?
	■ What impacts did these "surprises" have on project effectiveness, costs, and time?
Results	**Technical:**
	■ What results were obtained?
	■ How "good" were these results?
	Business:
	■ What results did the analyses yield?
	■ Is further work needed to obtain better results?
Conclusions	**Technical:**
	■ Can the results be directly applied to resolve the technical problem?
	■ What technical steps should be taken to implement these results?
	■ Has this research yielded other ideas for improving production that should be followed up in future research?
	Business:
	■ How can these results be integrated most effectively from a cost/time viewpoint?
	■ What impact will application of these results have on reducing rejection rates?
	■ Can this solution be applied to other production problems or to improve production in other areas?

Multi-task research report

For a research report on a large multi-task program, our organizational plan broadens into the following framework:

while a multi-task report may require expansion.

Needs, problems, and opportunities	From both technical and business viewpoints: ■ What needs prompted the company's investment in this research? ■ What problems had to be addressed? ■ What opportunities or benefits did the company stand to gain if the research project succeeded?
Scope and goals	■ What specific technical elements of the problem were covered?... and why? ■ What goals did the research attempt to achieve: • from a scientific viewpoint? • from a business viewpoint?

This section sets the stage for managers to digest the information in the "Solution" and "Results" sections.

Solution	■ What approach was selected to solve the specific problems and achieve the identified goals? • technical reasons • company business reasons ■ How did it compare to other possible approaches? • technical advantages and disadvantages • business advantages and disadvantages ■ What specific tasks did the research include? • technical steps • business-related tasks ■ What difficulties were encountered? How were they solved? • technical difficulties • administrative and other non-technical snags ■ What "shortcuts" or other unexpected advantages popped up in the course of the research that could be useful in other R&D projects?
Results	■ What results did each task yield? Interpret for the non-specialist manager. ■ From a scientific viewpoint, how "good and complete" were these results? ■ From a business view, how did these results compare with expectations—e.g., cost, schedules, staff performance.

Conclusion	On the basis of all the previous information: **Technical:** ■ To what extent did the research solve its targeted problems and achieve its intended goals? ■ What future scientific work should follow? ■ What other spinoffs or related research directions show promise? **Business:** ■ What impacts can the results have on the company?
Recommendations	**Technical:** ■ What future research in this or related areas should the company undertake? ■ What steps could be taken in future projects to prevent the difficulties encountered in this project and to improve results? ■ What actions should be taken in future projects to utilize the shortcuts and other efficiencies discovered during this project? **Business:** ■ What actions should the company take to utilize the results of this research? ■ What future investments should the company make in follow-up research in this area, or in related directions?

A complex proposal needs an implementation section (really an expanded solution section)...

Proposals[*]

For a long, complex industrial **proposal**, whether solicited or unsolicited, we can modify the expanded framework by adding an **implementation** section—in essence, a practical delineation of the solution section. We also need to expand the **problem** section by including more detailed and convincing information, especially on the benefits and opportunities the proposed research results might offer the company. The **solution** section should also be expanded to cover a discussion of alternative approaches to attacking the research problem. Such an explanation gives managers a broader perspective on the research options available and a better appreciation of the proposed method researchers selected.

On the other hand, we can likely contract the sections on results and conclusions.

Because **results** can only be anticipated in a proposal, this section should focus on how variations in timing and funding can impact the quality and utility of the results. Such explanations enhance decision making because they give company managers—or outside clients—a clearer picture of the proposed research's "risks and rewards".

---

[*] This proposal outline applies broadly to in-house proposals and to many proposals to companies by outside R&D firms. Solicited proposals, particularly government procurements, often request a different order of information and format. Sometimes other data may be required. However, the basic content suggested here should usually be included. In addition to responsiveness to the request for proposal, a proposal can be evaluated for content completeness by checking against the double-5 scheme.

The **conclusions** section also needs to be modified to cover the potential long-term benfits and tangible reports, products, and other assistance the "proposal requesters" will receive.

and modified, perhaps contracted, results and conclusions.

Clearly, researchers must orient the entire proposal to the specific needs and aims of their clients—whether in-house managers, or external proposal requesters.

Now, let's look at a typical proposal framework.

Needs, opportunities, and problems	In proposals, researchers need to detail all the technical and business reasons for the company—or client—to undertake a research effort. They should explain:

■ The **business needs** the research could fulfill—e.g., developing a new or superior product or production method; establishing a patent position

■ The **broad opportunities** and **benefits** that research results might offer the company—e.g., entering new markets; outperforming the competition; enlarging market share; improving manufacturing productivity; developing new products

■ The technical **problems** that need to be addressed. They should be listed—if possible—in order of importance.

Especially if the proposal responds to an outside request, this section must show an empathetic grasp of the research problem and purpose.

Scope and goals	**Technical:** Researchers must analyze and prioritize all the facets of the problem they propose to solve. If the problem is very broad, they may have to select and formulate the specific problem elements they propose to cover. Then they can set—and achieve—realistic goals.

Business: The goals and elements selected should be justified according to relevant criteria—for example, their significance in solving the problem as a whole, their cost-effectiveness, time to solution, and impact on other company activities.

Thus, the stage is ready to present the proposed solutions and their implementation.

Solution	■ What approach do researchers suggest as most likely to solve the selected problems and achieve the set goals?

    • How does it compare with other possible technical approaches?

    • What business advantages and disadvantages does it have?

■ What special requirements or difficulties are anticipated? How will they be handled?

    • Technical requirements, e.g., special equipment

    • Administrative or other non-technical needs.

Implementation	■ How will the project be organized technically? Into what tasks?

■ What researchers are slated to participate? What are their credentials? What specific responsibilities will each have?

■ How will the project be managed? What are the responsibilities of each member of the management team? What are their credentials?

■ What previous experience—and successes—have these researchers and project managers had in working as a team?

Implementation (continued)	■ What are the milestones, work plans, and overall schedules for the project?
	■ What are the anticipated costs for staff, equipment, services, overheads, "other" (e.g., travel)?
	■ How will these costs be spread over the project's duration?
	■ What quality-, cost-, and schedule-control measures will be implemented?
	■ How will the company or proposal requester benefit from this implementation plan?
Results anticipated	■ What level of technical results can reasonably be anticipated within the proposed staff, time, and cost parameters?
	■ What results could be anticipated under different parameters? —e.g., of time and budgets? enlarged staff? a phased approach? state-of-the-art equipment?
	■ What other factors could expedite or hamper the project's progress and results?
Conclusions	■ What **specific** help and benefit will the company or proposal requester derive from the research?
	■ What types and levels of conclusions are anticipated:
	• Technical conclusions
	• Business conclusions.
	■ What outputs will the research funders receive—and when? e.g.,
	• Progress reports
	• Final report
	• Oral presentation and discussion.
	■ What other "products" will the research yield? e.g.,
	• Prototype
	• Manual
	• Software
	■ Is a patent or licensing position likely to result?
	■ How will companies be able to use the results? Will project members assist in this process?
	■ If the research results are implemented, what are the long-term impacts? e.g., time to payback; return on investment.
Recommendations	■ What steps need to be taken to initiate the research? When?

Variations

The double-5 scheme lends itself to variations, as in this book:

▶

The basic double-5 scheme lends itself to other variations. For example, in this book, Chapter I deals with our survey **research**. It is therefore divided into the following sections:

• **Need**
• **Problem, scope, and goals**
• **Solution**
• **Results**
• **Conclusions**

The details of the survey results and the questionnaire are appended at the end of the book in Chapter VII.

From the perspective of the book as a whole, though,

Chapter I	deals with	**Problems** in researchers' technical/business writing and
		Scope and focus for the rest of the book
Chapters II and III	cover	**Solutions individual researchers and managers** can start implementing on their own
Chapter IV	covers	**Results** such actions can lead to
Chapter V	deals with	**Solutions companies—especially top management**—should initiate and support
Chapter VI	discusses	**Results and conclusions**—an outlook on broad writing improvement trends in industrial R&D.

Summary

To write a **summary** for a report, proposal, or other written communication, use the organizational scheme and highlights in each section as a foundation.

...and also facilitates writing a summary.

Thus, the double-5, problem-solving organizational approach can be used effectively as the basis for planning and writing almost any technical/business document.

Benefits of the organizational scheme

The power and appeal of this five-part approach lie in its logic: each part builds on the information and decisions from the preceding part. Thus, organizing and writing a convincing logical document depends on the quality of the first section: it must explain the needs, opportunities, and problems—both technical and business—that spur companies to invest in specific research areas.

In this scheme, each section builds logically on preceding sections.

Though researchers may not relish (and sometimes may even resent) explaining these business practicalities to managers, they need to remember that companies will only fund research—whether long- or short-term—if they see a payoff at the end of the road. And many times, only researchers are in a position to estimate and evaluate the technical success of these R&D efforts.

The scheme also spurs researchers to deal with R&D's business implications.

Researchers' reluctance to deal with business factors often stems from lack of information. If so, researchers need to contact others in the company—e.g., marketing, planning, or production staff—to fill in the business picture. This interface can be extremely beneficial: while it increases researchers' awareness of problems, needs, and capabilities in other segments of the company, it also educates non-research staff members about researchers' efforts and results, and about prospects for new products and processes. In fact, the current widespread use of **teams** with members from diverse technical and business areas encourages such interactions and speeds access to business information.

In short, our double-5 framework can result in several benefits. As we've already seen:

■ It can be used for almost all types of documents

■ It bridges the communications gap between researcher and manager.

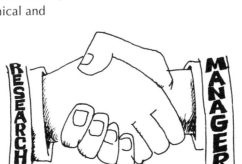

The benefits are significant:

But we'll also show that:

■ It provides a template for researchers to use in judging whether all needed types of information are included, especially the often-omitted conclusions and recommendations (see section on *Achieving focus, completeness, and logic* on page 35)

■ Likewise, it can help reveal holes in logic and information (same section, page 36)

■ It provides a basis for outlines that managers can use to quickly review prospective content, level of detail, and emphasis (see sections discussing **guidelines** and **feedback,** pages 79 to 82)

■ It provides managers and researchers an efficient framework for deciding how long a document should be (see the next section, *Deciding on—and writing at—the right level of technical detail*)

■ It facilitates reading and grasp for managers (see sections starting on pages 35 and 71)

■ As a prompter, it helps researcher overcome the "can't get started" syndrome we call "writer's block" (see the section on *Getting started*, page 37)

■ If used as a common denominator in a research group, it helps reduce large variation in researchers' output (see section on *Some tips on developing and using an outline*, page 40)

■ Ultimately, it can help cut the time researchers and managers devote to writing or reading (see sections relating to time management, pages 47 and 82).

Now we can look at other factors that influence content.

Deciding on—and writing at—the right level of technical detail

Need

A key content problem for researchers is determining the right level of technical detail.

Writing up information that readers don't need wastes the time of both author and audience. Before researchers begin to write, they must decide what level of technical detail to include.

Problem

But, how can researchers determine that "right" level of detail? First, by finding out:

■ **Who** the readers are

■ **How** these readers plan to use the document.

Thus, for example,

■ If the readers are **immediate managers and other scientists** who are familiar with the technical level of the research pursued, then more technical detail may be wanted. The reason? Precise details on how experimentation was conducted and how equipment was used may help these readers improve research efficiency and quality in other projects. For proposals, such details might also indicate the level or quality of potential results.

■ If the main readers are **managers responsible for long term R&D planning,** less technical detail may be needed. Instead, they may only want the critical highlights—e.g., the solution approaches that have been most successful, the results that have been most exciting, and the specific R&D areas that show the most promise for follow-up or spinoffs. However, sufficient detail must be included to enable these managers to make informed decisions on such long-range planning areas as R&D concentration, equipment purchases, and staffing.

■ **Managers responsible for product planning and manufacturing engineering** may become interested in greater detail as the research approaches the development stage.

■ **Executives** may, or may not, be interested beyond the first two or three levels of detail listed in the table on page 30. Many may only want to know the main technical concepts behind the research. But all are certain to want more detail on the business possibilities the research may offer.

Thus, when researchers know a document's readership and intended use, determining the required level of technical detail is relatively easy. To accurately meet the needs, researchers can—and should—discuss with their prospective readers, particularly their managers, the level of detail for each part of the document or even for each task. They should also clarify the amount and type of supporting documentation or data to include. Such clarifications should take place during document planning, before wasting time and effort on unnecessary writing.

Another straightforward indicator of the amount of detail needed is the prescribed length of a document. For example, if a multi-task proposal or project report is limited to three pages, it can probably include only a brief executive summary that is restricted to the top two levels of technical detail shown in our table.

However, the real headache begins when the readership is "multi-tiered", including managers from all the above groups. One option, not often practical, is to prepare separate documents targeted to needs and interests of the different groups of managers. But within one document, how can researchers respond effectively to such varying needs and backgrounds?

This level will depend on :

During document planning, discussions with managers about the level of detail they expect will expedite writing tasks.

The problem is more difficult when readers include several tiers of management, or other diverse audiences.

Solution

Here are some suggestions for handling this level-of-technical-detail problem. Fortunately, it's confined primarily to the "solution" and "results" sections.

First, a guiding principle: go from the general to the specific. The idea is to "ease" readers into the details they need and not plunge them into unfamiliar waters. As one manager wrote:

> "Specific interest and backgrounds of readers generally are varied...Writers too often assume the reader is as familiar with the subject as the writer, or totally remembers the contents in previous reports on the same subject."

Second, classify the levels of technical detail for the "Solution" section. Here's one way:

Level	Information included
1	General, brief description of the technical approach to solving the research problem
2	Outline of the subdivision of the general approach into specific tasks
3	General approach to solving each specific task
4	Details for solving each specific task.

A similar classification can be used to decide on the level of technical detail for reporting "Results".

Finally, some rules of thumb can also help researchers choose the right level of technical detail for their documents:

- Include only enough detail to meet the minimum needs of the identified readers
- Exclude minutely detailed supporting data from the body of the document; if needed, append them in a separate section at the end[*]
- Use examples, based on familiar experiences and general knowledge, to describe technical approaches, especially to non-specialists.[**]

Results

These suggestions for handling technical details can benefit both readers and writers:

- If the document proceeds from the general to the specific, readers can later follow through on as little—or as much—detail as they want (Level 1)
- If the general approach is subdivided into tasks (Level 2), readers can turn to the individual areas that interest them most (Level 3)
- If highly detailed supporting data are appended at the back rather than in the body of the document, all readers can better grasp the flow and trend of the technical solution and results. Those interested in fine details can turn to the appendices.

---

[*] Note that we've taken this advice ourselves: we've appended the details of the survey results at the end of this book.

[**] For other suggestions on handling level of detail for multi-tiered audiences, see the suggestions in *Using format to boost comprehension* on page 71.

■ If the body of the report is shortened, both readers and writers save time

■ If the technical details, especially the results, are taken from printouts and other already available outputs, the researchers' writing chores are reduced.

(As you can see, even in this section we've shortened the organizational scheme to "need-problems-solutions-results".)

Making documents more concise...and shorter

The words are often used interchangeably. But "concise" is not always equivalent to "short"; a document can be long and still be concise. Concise content, in our view, means excluding redundant, irrelevant, and unnecessary information.

To make documents more concise:

Here are a few ways to improve conciseness and reduce length.

Remove redundant information

Check your first, broad outline to make sure you aren't building in redundancies by covering the same topic more than once. (See page 40 on preparing outlines.) Then, review your detailed outline to make sure specific information isn't repeated, except where necessary for understanding. Also, evaluate whether you're rehashing the same information in a different guise. You can always refer the reader to a specific page or paragraph if you want to reinforce a point.

• remove redundant information (your outline will help)

With a good outline, it's faster and easier to spot actual or potential redundancies than with a first draft or a completed document.

However, a few words of caution:

■ The document summary, which should stand by itself, will obviously contain the main points that you expand upon later. It is not redundant.

■ A few main ideas may need to be repeated for emphasis.

■ A document can be too "information-dense". If you are too strict about not repeating an idea, the reader may miss the point altogether.

Remove irrelevant information

Recheck your detailed outline to spot irrelevant or unnecessary information. Then thoroughly discuss your outline with your manager to further pinpoint what information is—and isn't—needed. Watch out particularly for such items as:

• remove irrelevant information (e.g., too much detail on background, procedures, or results)

■ Unnecessarily detailed histories of the scientific background of a subject—e.g., what worker did a particular experiment in 1906. While this "background"

may be important in a paper for a scientific journal, it may not be needed in an industrial document. However, information that relates to work your competitors may be doing or to future market share for your company should be included.

■ Detailed descriptions of lab procedures

■ Overly detailed technical descriptions of results.

Reduce document length

• and reduce document length.

Even if you are sure the outline will lead to a concise document, you still may not know if your end product will be short enough. To relieve this uncertainty, check with the manager before you write a draft to get a rough estimate of how long the document should be. Suppose the manager expects a 5-page document and you estimate yours will turn out to be 20 pages. Here's what you can do:

Here are some approaches:

■ Review again whether you have indeed taken out unnecessary or redundant information.

■ Have a peer or an editor check for conciseness.

■ Delete details on lab work, but stress and interpret the main points of the results and your recommendations.

■ Use tables to condense comparative information (see page 72 for an example).

■ Recast your report as an expanded "executive summary". Append detailed data on results and lab work—even copies of printouts with brief explanations—at the end of the report. Then managers can easily decide whether or not to read them.

Or, consider writing an expanded executive summary and appending copies of the results.

We strongly suggest that managers and researchers look hard at this last, more extreme solution. Many respondents in our survey made similar suggestions. While it is not any easier to write a good summary than a good document, the starting point is different: researchers will likely spend far less time writing a 5-page summary and appending copies of actual results than agonizing over what details to include in a 20-page document.

After you are certain that you have excluded information redundancies and irrelevancies, and that the length is right, you can look at tightening the language. The section on *Style* (page 53) will give you some suggestions.

Attaining clarity

First we'll define "clarity", and then look at how to achieve it.

Clarity—writing so the meaning cannot be misunderstood—is difficult to attain,

Clarity means that what you write is unambiguous—it can have only one meaning. However, of all the qualities researchers try to attain—and that managers most request—it is the most elusive. In fact, researchers may never be able to achieve perfect clarity in writing about R&D because the material is often new and difficult. But they can take steps to improve the readers' chances of understanding the precise intent.

What elements improve clarity? Certainly those we have discussed above—good organization, correct level of detail, and conciseness. However, from a content viewpoint, certain factors are particularly important for conveying information clearly.

but is enhanced by:

Here are some suggestions.

Introduce information in a logical, expected sequence

Two terms are especially important here, both for the overall organization of a document and its individual parts: logical and expected sequence. When a writing task starts, researchers and managers need to stop thinking in terms of "introduction, body, end" and start thinking in terms of "problem, scope, solution, results, conclusion". Once this logical organizational pattern has been accepted and ingrained, researchers will have a clearer concept of the necessary content at the outset—and an easier time preparing their material. Managers will also have a clear pattern in mind when they read information—and will thus have an easier time finding the information they want. Remember: when information does not appear in an "expected sequence", readers' attention is diverted to puzzling over such questions as, "Does this information belong here?", or, even worse, "Does this information really belong at all?". Such surprises in sequence undermine clear understanding of the material and waste the reader's time.

• using a logical and expected order—don't surprise the reader

This organizational principle also applies to each segment of a document, from chapters all the way down to paragraphs. As much as possible, setting up each chapter on a problems-solution-results basis reinforces the "expected sequence" idea and improves clarity.

Present general principles before going into detail

Although this suggestion seems obvious (and is discussed on page 30 under *Deciding on—and writing at—the right level of technical detail*), it is amazing how often researchers jump into the minutest technical details without first describing, even briefly, the concept or principle underlying the research.

This seemingly simple guideline is not always easy to follow, for several reasons:

■ The material may be very complex and may not lend itself easily to generalizations.

■ The general principle, itself, even when identified, may be difficult to simplify or to articulate in non-technical terms.

■ Researchers often fear that generalizations may not represent their work accurately enough.

■ Researchers are often so engrossed in their work that it is hard for them to identify exactly what principle—or level of principle—managers need to understand first before they can cope with the rest of the detail. As several

• presenting general principles before details.

Though this advice may be hard to follow because:

managers noted, and as we have often seen, researchers tend to assume readers have much more knowledge of a particular area than is actually the case.

■ Researchers' reports and proposals may be reviewed or read by several levels of management—from immediate project and department managers, to executives deciding on the future of the firm's R&D. The further away from the immediate manager, the more sketchy that manager's knowledge of the research area is likely to be. Thus, researchers have a difficult problem: what may be clear and completely understandable for one set of managers may be unclear and hard to understand for another set.

The solutions to such difficulties are not easy. But here are some ideas researchers can try to apply. (We have used them extensively in our publications.)

there are some ways to apply it: ▶

■ The argument that "you can't always find a generalization" is often an excuse. Even if the technical details are complex, there is always at least one principle, concept, or idea underlying a particular direction of research. So, despite the difficulty, researchers must provide this basis. One researcher told us his professor used to claim, "If you can't explain the principle in terms that intelligent people can understand, you probably don't really understand it yourself..."

To overcome their fears of inaccurate generalizations, researchers can introduce caveats, or slightly "hedge" their statements. (But beware of over-hedging, as discussed on page 62.) Then, other scientists will have less reason to criticize; and managers will gain a better perspective.

■ Another way to improve the clarity of a generalization is to give an example or to use and analogy. For example, researchers could add... "This principle is something like XYZ" (some well known technical rule that all readers know and understand).

■ Use simple diagrams to replace long, difficult descriptions of equipment, procedures, and results. Sometimes a diagram can clarify information more quickly and accurately than a thousand well selected words. For example, the figure here shows a **"ghost" cellular carrier cell,** a novel drug delivery system.

Other methods to handle clarity problems for readers with different levels of technical background are discussed next under *Facilitating reading and grasp* and under *Deciding on—and writing at—the correct level of technical detail* (page 28). Ways to increase clarity from a format view are covered on page 71.

Helping researchers write...

Facilitating reading and grasp

To make your document easier to read and understand:

■ Prepare a useful, comprehensive table of contents

■ Use your outline as the basis for a table of contents, with sufficient subheadings to immediately show the logical sequence

■ Use the chapter headings as page "headers" to show readers where they stand as they progress in their reading

■ Write headings that describe what you are actually discussing. For example, if you are writing a final report on project Eureka, instead of writing "Introduction" and other non-informative headings, use headings and subheadings such as:

Why project Eureka was conducted at Acme company

Technical reasons

- Quality control problems with rotors, stators, and bearings
- Wear problems with rotors and bearings
- Tighter specifications required for stators by industrial customers

Business reasons

- Work under way at competitors
- Expected new product appearances
- Expected changes in demand

Potential benefits the project could offer

- _____
- _____

*To facilitate **reading and grasp,** you can:*

Achieving focus, completeness, and logic

Focus means that the attention of the reader is guided to the important ideas in the document. It means that less important, but related, ideas are relegated to less important positions so that attention is not diverted to peripheral information. Thus, focused documents can sharply communicate complex information to readers.

All the elements we have discussed so far—good organization, conciseness, appropriate level of technical detail, and clarity—help improve the focus of a document...almost by default: if unnecessary detail and irrelevant information are eliminated, the focus immediately becomes sharper.

However, to address readers' needs more precisely, researchers need to remember that each section of the organizational framework deals with a specific area of information. Though we have stressed the principle of including each segment of our framework in a technical/business document, information in certain parts may be more important and useful to managers than that in others. Thus, in their discussions with managers during the document planning stage, researchers should try to pinpoint the sections or specific topics that need to be emphasized. Researchers can then tailor the depth of attention and detail of information in each section according to readers' requirements.

Focus—directing attention to important ideas—is enhanced by careful organization, conciseness, level of detail, clarity...

...and consistent emphasis on meeting readers' needs.

Alternatively, managers may be interested in a specific orientation—for example, the impact of the research on a particular product or market. This focus should then be consistently maintained throughout the document.

To see whether the outline or draft is **complete**, researchers working on a report, for example, can ask themselves:

▶ ■ Are all the content elements covered:

- Are all the problems and needs stated?
- Does the scope reflect the main points of the problem?
- Does the solution really solve the problem? If not, is it clear what parts are (or are not) addressed?
- Are the results given for each research task?
- Are all the conclusions from the results addressed?
- Are recommendations for further action included?

■ For each section, are the business as well as the technical implications and interpretations included?

*...as can the **logic** of a document.*

The organizational framework also helps ensure that the document is **logical**. Researchers can check logic by asking such questions as:

▶ ■ Are the problems, needs, and opportunities stated in the opening section addressed in the rest of the document, especially in the "scope and goals" and the "solutions" sections?

■ Does the "solutions" section respond to the problems specified in the "scope and goals" section?

■ Do the "results" indeed follow from the work descriptions in the "solutions" section?

■ Are the results interpreted? One manager noted: ..."Often they (researchers) simply say what was done, not why, and not what this result means!!"

■ Do all the conclusions and recommendations follow from previous information? Or are some of the conclusions drawn without support in the document?

■ Are goal attainments evaluated in the "conclusions" section?

■ Do the scientific results translate into suggested research actions in the "recommendations" section? One manager wrote he needs to know "What decision issues are pending? What actions do I need to take?"

■ Do the "opportunities" (described in the first section) materialize as concrete business suggestions in the "recommendations" section?

■ Is the document consistent in order, tables, figures, lists, and terminology throughout? (This question of consistency will be discussed in detail in the section on *Style: Language and format* starting on page 53.)

A non-partisan reviewer may evaluate logic and completeness better than the writer.

Researchers often have difficulty in checking completeness and logic because of their intense familiarity with the subject. Review by a colleague, manager, or editor who is less involved in the work usually helps.

Strategies for writing*

This section suggests ideas to make writing more productive and efficient. It covers three key areas:

- Getting started
- Writing the first draft...and fine-tuning it
- Writing efficiently...or...solving the lack-of time problem.

Getting started

How hard is it to get started writing? Listen to what one scientist said:

> "A major difficulty I have is the initial stages of **starting a major document** (emphasis ours): How to approach it, how to organize data, what to include, how to proceed. I often find that I 'stew' about it subconsciously for a number of days before the ideas 'click' in my head—and only then can I begin to write productively. If I try to force it before that point, I usually wind up with a number of false starts or drift from the topic at hand to other topics that are also competing for attention. It would be great to find ways to **speed up the initial organizing/conceptualization process**, so I could organize my ideas more quickly and less painfully."

Ways to help get started

The truth is, there is no magic formula that can suddenly convert research into a well organized, well written communication. It's hard work to conceive, implement, and refine a good piece of writing.

But there are ways to stimulate the process of getting started and overcoming proverbial "writer's block".

The first, critical step is to **plan** the document. Several approaches can be used, some more structured than others. But all planning strategies should have two points in common:

- They should result in a comprehensive, well-organized outline
- They should encourage use of "prewriting" planning time for free-range, creative thinking.

Researchers will have to discover the method—or combination of methods—that works best for them. Our aim is to suggest ideas that can lead to an improved planning strategy.

One approach is to prompt or "artificially induce" a basic outline of the document.[4] You can do this prompting by asking a series of questions based on our double-5 organizational scheme.

Getting started is always tough, as one writer attests:

*But without careful **planning,** it's even tougher.*

*One planning approach **prompts an outline** through a series of questions based on our organizational scheme.*

SOMETIMES YOU JUST GOTTA GET YOUR BATTERY CHARGED!

TRY THE DOUBLE 5 SURE STARTER

---

* This section was formerly called "Procedures for Writing".

For example, if you are writing a research report, you should first ask:

- **Who** will **read** this report?
- How do they need to use this report?
- Therefore, what is the **title**—the **main focus**—of the document?

Write your answers down. Then you can start your outline by working your way through the questions in the five-part scheme for organizing a report. Note that they follow the basic pattern shown on page 22.

Here's how the questions will produce an outline for a research report.

▶

Problem	■ What **problems, needs, or opportunities** did the research address?
	■ What **benefits** did my company (or client) expect to receive from this work—both long- and short-term?
Scope and Goals	■ How did I define the scope of the work? Or what **goals** did I expect this work to achieve?
	■ Why were these specific goals important to the company and to the work?
Solution	■ What approach to **solving** these problems or fulfilling these needs did I select?
	■ Why was this approach preferable to others? (You might make a table comparing several approaches; it would show the relative advantages or disadvantages for the company at a glance.)
	■ What main tasks did I conduct? To help the reader, list these tasks in logical or developmental order; this listing will not necessarily conform with the order of performance.
	■ What significant comments can I make on the conduct of the work that would be useful in future R&D or business evaluations? For example, was the work completed "on time", or did certain difficulties crop up that required more time to resolve? Or, how effectively did some new equipment work? (Other R&D groups may be very interested.)
Results	■ What main **results** did I achieve? Try to match them with the list of tasks mentioned above.
	■ What business implications do these results have? e.g., Were the expected results achieved?
Conclusions	■ What scientific—and business—**conclusions** can I reach? Where is the research going? What are the long-term implications of the research?
	■ What **recommendations** can I make to enhance R&D progress and to further the company's business goals? For example, what are the next steps the company should take, from both technical and business viewpoints?

For a proposal, you would ask similar questions phrased in terms of what you **expect** to achieve. But your emphasis would shift. You would also need to ask questions on how you expect to implement the work you are proposing. (See page 25 for a basic list of questions.) But most important, you have to remember to ask yourself, "What unique or special contributions can I offer that benefit the proposal receiver?"

For memos and other business correspondence, this approach—once honed—can expedite writing. You need to ask yourself such questions as:

■ What is the problem or issue?

■ What steps should be—or have been—taken to resolve it?

■ What actions will—or should—result?

Then you can add a "Hello" and a "thank you" ...and you're almost done.

This "prompting" approach may work well to help some researchers get started—particularly the more analytically inclined. It may be especially suitable for researchers working alone on reports or memos. By the time all the questions have been answered, the basic elements of the outline are already **written**...and organized. Now, researchers can continue by expanding, revising, and fine tuning each part according to the specific purpose.

A second approach—the complete reverse of our first suggestion—is to use a "braindump". Here, either an individual or a group writes down, **without critiquing**, any and all ideas that might be included in the document.[*]

This method maximizes the free-wheeling atmosphere; it just requires that the ideas deal with the broad subject under discussion. Thus, it is never limited to a specific question or subset of ideas. For researchers whose creative thinking is associative rather than analytical, this may be an excellent route for getting started. For proposal writing—when a group wants to hammer out innovative ideas for solving a problem or responding to a need—this method may be ideal.

*See reference 4 for a discussion on idea generation methods.

The same approach, with some adjustments, works for proposals, or memos.

An alternative is a "braindump"—generating ideas without critiquing.

This freewheeling approach may be ideal for innovative group efforts—especially proposals;

NOW DON'T LAUGH... 'CAUSE THIS IS RIGHT OFF THE TOP OF MY HEAD!... BUT, WHAT IF....

but reviewing and screening the ideas can be a lengthy process.

However, the process of organizing a comprehensive outline after such a session can be protracted. First, the individual or group needs to review the long list of ideas generated during the braindump and plug them into the various parts of the organizational scheme. Then, the ideas need to be screened for relevance to the document readers' criteria. In addition, further brainstorming may be needed to balance each section, yet create a focused, comprehensive document.

*A **hybrid approach,** combining these two, can also be effective.*

A third approach is a hybrid of the first two: **brainstorm each double-5 section.** This attack can work well for many individuals; it can also work well in a group because the questions leave plenty of room for generating, discussing, and writing down ideas.

This procedure has an important advantage: its net result is an **organized set of topics** with points that can readily be screened and converted into a comprehensive outline. It can provide an efficient way to elicit and integrate creative ideas. Thus, it's a good starter.

Some tips on developing and using an outline

Where should you **start planning an outline**? A good case can be made for starting "at the beginning": it helps you keep on track and keep out pet irrelevancies. But, if you feel strongly about a certain section or know clearly what you want to say, begin the outline there; then back up to the beginning and continue down to the end. Just make sure that all the remaining sections of the outline are logical and consistent with the first one you wrote.

As you plan an outline, no matter where you start, make sure it is logical and consistent.

After you've listed all the points you want to include in a section, you'll need to organize them in a logical sequence, including "major headings" with subsumed ideas. The classical procedure to prepare such an outline is to indent each succeeding level of subheading further to the right; or to number them1, 1.1, 1.1.1, etc. You can choose any method that works for you or invent your own, as long as it provides a shorthand organizing method that is consistent.

Use the proper tools to prepare an outline. One technique some researchers like uses a large sheet of unlined paper divided into columns.* We recommend assigning a column for each of the main parts of our organizational scheme (Problem, Scope and Goals, Solution, Results, Conclusions). Write in the main

One technique uses a large sheet that lets you see the whole outline at a glance.

* This technique has been taught for many years at the Battelle in-house courses given by Dolores Landreman, a former senior proposal writer.[5]

Problem	Scope/Goals	Solution	Results	Conclusions

technical and business points at the top of each column; then expand on each of these points in list form. For long outlines, you can use several sheets of paper and put them up on the wall.

The value of this technique: you can see the whole outline at a glance. This overview helps you quickly catch redundancies, irrelevancies, inconsistencies, and gaps in logic.

An alternative to the "large-sheet" approach is to outline right on the computer. The advantage: you can easily delete or move headings, revise on the spot, and print out a clean outline that is easy to follow. But expect to fine tune or add headings as your writing—and thinking—progress. Leave space for handwritten insertions; or revise the outline on the computer.

Or, you can outline on the computer...

A more sophisticated approach uses the "outline views" or mode in many word processing programs. These software aids can help you develop an outline in any degree of detail. You can also quickly view different versions of the outline: "collapsed" (main headings) or "expanded" (main plus subheadings). You can even write text at each level. Then, if you move an item in the outline, the accompanying text also moves.

even using special software.

EXPANDED

```
+  MANAGING A QUALITY IMPROVEMENT PROGRAM
   +  Increased productivity through quality improvement
      +  Historical Perspective on Quality Improvement
      +  Quality Improvement Philosophies
      +  Quality Improvement Programs
   +  A Plan for Managing a Quality Improvement Program
      +  Introduction
      +  The Steering Committee
      +  Program Overview
      +  Resource Requirements
   +  Training and Educational Needs
      +  Program Roles and Educational
      +  Training Materials
   +  Program Implementation - Quality
      -  Selecting the Process
      +  Formation of QIT
      +  Getting Started
      +  The Steps Toward Process Imp
   +  Technical Support - Problem Sol
      Statistical Methods
      +  Problem Solving Techniques
         managing a quality improvem
```

COLLAPSED

```
+  MANAGING A QUALITY IMPROVEMENT PROGRAM
   +  Increased productivity through quality improvement
   +  A Plan for Managing a Quality Improvement Program
   +  Training and Educational Needs
   +  Program Implementation - Quality Improvement Teams
   +  Technical Support - Problem Solving Techniques and
      Statistical Methods
   +  Program Evaluation and Coordination
   +  Looking to the future
```

With suitable equipment to project material from the computer terminal to a large screen, groups can also use such software to develop outlines—adding, deleting, or regrouping headings as they wish. Then they can print out and distribute an ordered version of the outline, complete with all headings, and a Table of Contents.

This technique is particularly attractive for large planning groups.

Be prepared to **spend enough time—and it may be considerable—to fully develop a satisfactory outline before you begin writing**. The temptation (and pressure) to wrap up the outline and start writing is always strong. But with the whole document spread out before you in outline form, your ability to globally view and think about the relative emphasis and logical fit of each part is far superior. Extra time spent on the outline will save you significant amounts of writing time. It will focus your attention on the main issues of content, rather than details of style.

Do not start writing until you have a satisfactory outline; you'll gain in many ways.

Further, if several researchers are writing individual portions of the document, a comprehensive, well defined, and clearly understood outline is absolutely essen-

A complete, detailed outline developed before writing begins...will enable you to produce a better final document, faster.

But ultimately, the outline—which may run from a simple organizational scheme to topic sentences or even paragraphs—

must prove useful in the writing process.

The safest place to start writing a draft is at the beginning—you might avoid unnecessary revision later.

While writing is still done with pencil and paper, the disadvantages are costly:

tial. Because the interdependency of the authors is much higher, they have much less flexibility for revising or juggling information during the writing stage. Planning the outline as a group helps assure common understanding that enables researchers to follow the outline better. It also helps reduce the tremendous variations of different researchers' input to multi-authored documents.

How much of an outline do you need before starting to write the first draft? The answer varies with the individual. Some researchers expand a main-word outline almost to the paragraph level. Others use the briefest of outlines just to keep them on track—perhaps little more than our organizational scheme of problem, scope and goals, solution, results, and conclusion.

Some researchers use a good compromise between these extremes: they think of the outline as an expanded table of contents. First, the outline serves a dual purpose, saving the time and trouble of setting up a whole table of contents. Second, developing a table of contents gives researchers an opportunity to think about how readers will use the document and to write headings that will enhance the readers' grasp (see page 35 for an example.).

Whatever route you choose, you must start by planning and outlining your document. Our experience has proven over and over: the better and more comprehensive the outline, the better the final document and the faster it can be completed.

But the final test of a good outline is its usefulness in the actual writing process—our next subject for discussion.

Writing the first draft...and fine-tuning it

True, once the outline is done, the ice is broken; the writing process is started. But writing the first draft is the most difficult task most researchers face.

Researchers frequently ask where to start the writing once the outline is completed. One answer is: "Start with the section that interests you most." This approach is natural for group writing; obviously, participants will write the sections based on their expertise. But it may lead to inefficiencies.

Starting at the beginning is certainly safer. This suggestions stems from experience. For example, in the course of fleshing out the "Problems, Needs, and Benefits" section, or defining the "Goals", you may discover that changes are needed in the rest of the document. If you have already written some sections (say, the "Solutions" and "Implementation" section of a proposal) you'll have to spend additional time revising them. However, if you start writing at the beginning, the revisions needed downstream can be made in the outline first.

But wherever you start, here are some ideas for writing that first draft—then revising and editing it—more quickly. They're divided into two categories: "Using pencil and paper—compared to other alternatives", and "Using the computer".

Using pencil and paper—compared to other alternatives

This "pencil + paper + secretary to input drafts" procedure, though less widely used in 1993 than in 1985, has serious disadvantages:

■ Writing by hand is time consuming One researcher[*] has estimated that it takes twice as long to "compose" handwritten than computer-generated copy, even for "three-finger keyboarders".

* Personal communication with researchers in office automation group at Battelle, 1985.

■ Someone else needs to "key in" the draft on the computer; and typing from handwritten copy engenders mistakes.

■ Revising is time consuming. The researcher usually reads the printout and marks revisions. Then the secretary has to incorporate these corrections into a new version.

■ This slow process may continue through several cycles.

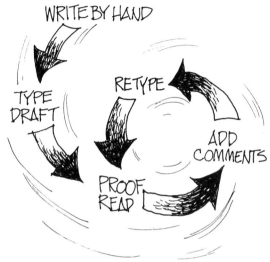

Throughout this process, further delays are introduced because the word processing operator is busy typing or revising drafts for others. Besides, with this method, it's hard to legibly insert, delete, or move material. Using an eraser (several researchers called it a major tool!) often muddies the draft and makes it even harder to read.

Even word processing operators do not always speed up document production. While the actual time to make revisions may be shorter, the queue of researchers waiting to have their documents keyed-in and revised may be longer. The reason: managers often justify the costs of installing a group's new computer by downsizing secretarial staff.

Therefore, our suggestions are:

■ Researchers can use a tape recorder to generate drafts for transcription. A few already do because it speeds first draft preparation. This method, though, means learning how to use the tape recorder effectively; it requires practice. Researchers must precisely follow an outline, articulate well, spell out difficult technical words, and indicate clearly where changes are needed.

■ Researchers can generate their own drafts on the computer. This alternative, by far the most efficient and flexible, can significantly shorten and streamline the writing process.

Using the computer

Writing the first draft

Once you're satisfied with your outline, **start composing your draft directly on the computer:** sit down, follow the outline rigorously, and write just as it comes.

Do not "write and scratch". **Do not** go back and revise while you are in this initial creative process of "getting it out...and on to paper". One researcher put it this way:

As alternatives, researchers can:

• *dictate on a tape recorder for transcription later*

• *generate drafts on a computer—by far the most efficient and flexible approach.*

Follow the outline;

let the writing flow out—do not "revise as you go".

"I try too hard to make the first draft the final draft. (I) spend too much time trying to get everything perfect the first time rather than simply getting the idea down and doing the refining later."

Our reasons for this advice:

- The flow of thought and logic tends to be better.
- It's faster than writing and scratching.
- You can still handle "great ideas" you get during the writing process.

In one sense, writing "straight through" according to the outline tests the soundness of an outline. But remember that your prime purpose in this initial writing is to **get down all the information** the document should have, in a logical framework. If, in the process of writing, you find the logic is becoming muddy or some information gaps are appearing, that's a signal you need to go back and rework the outline.

This approach lets you concentrate on substance, not style.

"Writing and scratching"—rather than "writing straight through"—has a major drawback: it tends to make the writer digress from the main issues and concentrate on small details. It tends to pull attention away from the substance and toward style—clearly two different levels of viewing the material.

If you get irresistible new ideas while you're writing, you don't have to forget about them. Just jot them down or key them in parenthetically as they occur.

New ideas can be added to the outline or keyed into a note for later insertion.

Important ideas to include…

Then continue where you left off. When you've completed the draft, you can go back, gather these ideas, consider if you really want to include them, and decide precisely where they belong.

Write the summary only **after** you have finished writing the document. Then, use your final outline, probably revamped through several iterations during the writing process, as a basis for your summary.

For the briefest of summaries (almost an abstract), write a sentence for each section. To expand slightly, write a short paragraph for each section. For an executive summary, include more business information in each section. Also, expand the vital data on the sections that require the most emphasis.

Reviewing, revising, and editing

Once you've completed the first draft, you can start reviewing, revising, and editing it. Divide this work into four steps:

Revising this first draft is a four-step process:

1. Review content, organization, and logic to be sure you've included all the needed information in **all** sections. Check whether the length is reasonable. Evaluate whether your draft closely approximates the information and ideas you want to convey. But, on the first pass through your manuscript, **revise to improve content issues only.**

2. On the second pass, edit the language; make it clear and concise.

3. Then decide on a format (e.g., page layout, heading weights, typeface, type size, page numbers, and headers or footers): follow it consistently. Lay out the pages of your document, inserting the tables and figures as close as possible to the text.

4. Finally, proofread for "mechanics"—e.g., spelling, punctuation, capitalization, matching of text and figures, agreement between the table of contents and actual page numbers.

Dividing the revision and editing process into these steps is efficient because it builds in review checkpoints that prevent "rejects" or massive "redos" at the end. Also, you can get specialized help to shorten your task and to improve the **quality** of your document.

For **Step 1**, you, of course, need to review the document first. But you should also ask a colleague or a manager to review it for content to be sure the information you included is useful, logical, complete, concise and clear for the reader. Warn reviewers not to get bogged down by details of spelling and format. A good editor, as an objective communicator, can also help review for organization and readability.

During the first step, find another reviewer, then revise and integrate comments as needed.

After such reviews, especially of major documents, be prepared for another whole "write-review-integrate-revise" cycle. Suggestions and questions from reviewers often spur new ideas for improvements...a sort of "document maturation" process.

For **Step 2**, first look at the language yourself. The section beginning on page 53 gives some editorial tools you can apply. Even if you are not very adept at first, trying to self-edit your writing will **increase your awareness** of trouble spots. As your experience gradually builds, your "language habits" will also improve.

Check language (step 2) yourself, but also try to get an editor's help and advice.

Here you can definitely use a technical editor. But ask the editor **why** certain changes were made; find out how they improved the document. Add this knowledge to your own bag of tricks.

In **Step 3**, you may not always have a choice: sometimes certain format guidelines are predetermined—e.g., size of page, columns, heading weights, or type size. Some companies, and some clients, prescribe a format. But, if you can choose, we strongly advise asking a designer or editor for assistance in formatting a document so that readers can digest information more easily. Today's word processing and desktop publishing programs can quickly produce professional-looking copy. (See also our suggestions on *Using format to boost comprehension* on page 71.)

Outside help is also useful in step 3, decisions on format.

In **Step 4**, after the document is edited for content and style, and formatted, it still needs one last review to make sure it has all come together consistently and correctly—e.g., the figures are all in the right place and marked accurately; the spelling and punctuation are correct; the headings are all the right weight...in short, a careful proofreading. Whether an editor, proofreader, or secretary needs to do this task depends largely on:

Step 4—the final check—can be delegated to an editor, proofreader, or secretary, depending on the specific document.

■ The document's importance

■ The individual's capabilities

■ The document's length, difficulty, and intended readership

■ Available time and funding.

Although this task can be delegated to others, you need the final say.

If suitable editorial help is available, the editor can assume responsibility during Step 1 and "shepherd" your document through all these phases, reviewing it with

However, use the computer advantageously:

- *compose on the computer and then easily revise and update*

you at critical points. This practice relieves you of many duties, for which you may lack time and training; it transfers these tasks to professionals who can do them better, faster, and cheaper. We'll discuss ways to use editorial help in more detail under *Tips for saving time* on page 47 and *Hire a technical editor* on page 86.

But, use the computer advantageously.

1. Originate or "compose" on the computer. Now, substantive revisions are so easy to make—for example, adding material, moving material to improve logical sequence, expressing a thought more accurately or clearly—even the first draft is often a superior product. You are no longer plagued by the constant errors, iterations, and irritations that arise from making corrections and having another person trying to decipher and execute them.

- *print out the draft for review and correction*

  or

  send it electronically for review

2. Print out the draft, and mark corrections by hand, if you like. This procedure offers the advantages of reviewing and revising a document at your convenience anywhere, not necessarily at the computer. Others can also review draft copies. Alternatively, send the draft electronically to reviewers; they too can comment electronically—without running hard copy.

3. For revisions, choose from two main options: Revise on the computer yourself, or give the marked copy and disk to a computer operator. When you update your own work, you simultaneously review, refine revisions, proofread, and cut iterations. You eliminate the wait for a word processing operator. But you may not make the revisions as efficiently. Using an operator, on the other hand, saves you direct revision time. Sometimes you can use a combination of these options. For example, do all the main content revisions of the early drafts yourself on the computer—but have a word processing operator do the later language changes and the final formatting.

- *make all revisions to generate a final draft, or have a word processing operator insert revisions.*

Because it often takes more than 50 percent of the budgeted time to move a document from initial assignment to completed first draft, the time saved via the computer vastly increases writing efficiency. That's also why we emphasize the advantage of a higher quality first draft: it potentially reduces document production time for all participants in the writing process—researchers, reviewers, computer operators, and editors. Thus, computers can significantly help improve document quality, reduce costs, and lessen researchers' frustration. With their improved writing productivity, researchers can devote more time to scientific work.

Use of the computer can improve writing efficiency, reduce costs, increase quality—and reduce frustration.

But let's look at what researchers have to say:

> "The single most important factor in improving my writing is the personal computer with word processing software. All other items pale before this—the ability to revise, change, and improve both content and grammar."

> "My output would probably be half as much and of much lower quality without direct access to computer-based word processing."

> "The personal computer with the right word processing options is the best thing since the calculator."

> "The computer has eliminated my fear of writing, revising, and editing."

> Q.E.D.

Writing efficiently...or... solving the lack of time problem

Insufficient time to write a quality document has emerged as the most serious obstacle researchers face. Clearly, this problem cannot be solved just by teaching researchers how to improve their writing skills and strategies. Rather, managers and researchers must cooperatively look at these time management difficulties and decide together on workable solutions. We'll discuss some options in the next chapter on *Steps managers can take*. For now, let's look at what researchers can do to alleviate the time crunch.

How can researchers handle their biggest problem—too little time to write?

Tips for saving time

Here are some tips you can apply right away. Some of these ideas may already be in your kit; others may seem difficult to use. But all of them derive from our experience.

To put these tips in context, suppose you are writing a final report on a research project.

As a researcher, you can try to:

Find out precisely what your "customer" wants...before you begin writing! (We repeat this advice because it's so vital.) Your customer may be your manager or

• *determine reader needs*

another internal or external client. Especially important: find out what parts of the work should be emphasized. Then you won't waste time writing unneeded information.

Don't reinvent the wheel. Before you started the project, you (or somebody) proposed it. Get out the proposal and use the "Problems, Needs, and Benefits" and the "Goals" sections as the basis for the first two parts of your report. Similarly, use the proposal's "Solutions" section as the basis for outlining your report's "Solutions" section. If changes during the research caused you to redefine these sections, you will have to adapt them. But you'll have a headstart because you won't be starting from scratch.

Develop the outline EARLY. Prepare the outline at the **beginning** of the research. Include your manager and future editor (if you have one!) at this stage. Then, as you complete each research task, write it up. If you can't write the report until the whole project is completed, at lest amend your early-developed outline as the work proceeds.

Several managers we spoke with recommend this "early start" approach; but all admit that most researchers do not use it. Though the reasons are understandable—pressure to continue other tasks on schedule, a previous report still on the docket, and so on—an enormous loss in efficiency (and possibly even in useful reporting) accrues by not writing up individual research tasks as they are completed.

- *use the original proposal as a headstart for writing a report*

- *prepare an outline early and write as research progresses*

Divide the outline into "timed-tasks". Before you start the first draft, divide your outline into tasks; match these tasks to the realistic blocks of time they require. Then set goals for writing the pieces of outline into a first draft. You need to decide what those time blocks are: if you can't get away for 2 or 3 days of concentrated work, arrange for 2- or 3-hour blocks.

- *schedule writing tasks to match realistic, available blocks of time*

However, try to schedule these work sessions close together. Otherwise, whenever you sit down to write, you waste time "catching up" to where you left off. In fact, spreading writing jobs over a long period is one of the biggest problems we run into—and a major cause of inefficiency. It also contributes to lack of flow

Helping researchers write...

and coherence in the final product. Further, try to schedule your writing blocks for the time of day when you're most productive.

Protect your time. Utilize all the usual "time-management tricks" to protect your writing time:

• *aggressively manage your time, e.g.,*
◄

- Ask your secretary to hold your calls and tell callers you'll get back to them at a certain time. Or, let your answering machine or voice mail collect your messages.

- Display a "Do not disturb until _____ o'clock" note.

- Notify colleagues and staff of your strict new schedule for *x* number of days.

- Keep an extra cup of coffee in your office so no one can grab you in the hall when you go for a refill.

- Have all your data and writing equipment on hand when you start.

- Arrange flextime schedules, if you can, so you can work without fear of interruption.

- Don't initiate any telephone calls (unless they're related to the writing, of course!)

Dedicate this time to your writing job.

This time-block planning for writing has several advantages:

so that:
◄

- You can still stay in the flow of work, because time is left during the day to return phone calls or attend urgent meetings.

- You can get work done in realistic time blocks. Also, reserving defined periods of time is practical, while allowing whole days for your writing tasks might be very difficult (or even impossible).

- You can maintain a higher level of concentration and creativity. In truth, are you consistently creative over longer periods? Don't you take a break after 2 or 3 hours anyway?

Delegate work. after you are satisfied with the content of your report, delegate as much of the follow-up editorial and production work as possible. This advice is sometimes hard for researchers to accept because a sense of ownership, or a lack of confidence in someone else's editorial capabilities, makes "letting go" hard. But, competent professionals can indeed save researchers time by:

• *get help for:*
◄

- Reviewing and editing the report for organization, clarity, and style

- Checking the report for compliance with customers' requests

- Meshing the input of several researchers

- Suggesting and designing graphics and tables

- Proofreading

- Checking for consistency of terms, in text, tables, and diagrams

- "Producing" the report—i.e., guiding it through all the draft and production stages, getting your approval only at certain critical points.

Some companies have in-house groups that can provide theses services. Other firms may have help within their departments or may retain outside firms or consultants. If your company offers such services, find and use them.

Prepare a realistic schedule based on the total time needed to complete the report

Estimate the time for writing the first draft

To plan a realistic writing schedule allocate 2 to 3 hour blocks of time to cover discrete sections or subsections of your detailed outline.

Dividing your outline into 2- to 3-hour blocks can help you estimate more realistically how long it will take you to write the first draft. However, your outline must have enough detail, both in headings and subheadings, before you can usefully divide it into these time blocks. If you just look at the main chapters and assign time, for example:

"Section 1—Problems, Needs, and Benefits— 1 block

"Section 2—Goals—1/2 block"...etc.,

you will almost certainly underestimate the amount of time they require.

Another way of planning your writing time is to estimate how many pages each section should have. Since this estimate is dictated by the relative importance of each section, it provides a guideline for allocating writing time. However, the ratio may not be direct. For example, a "Solutions" section may take five times as many pages as the "Problems" section; but the "Problems" section may also be far more difficult to write. Thus, more than five times the number of hours will need to be assigned. Planning by number of pages can also help determine the level of technical detail. (See example on page 51.)

So, if you want a fast, but realistic, time estimate for the first draft, follow this rule of thumb: allow twice the amount of time you "normally" would. And double or triple that amount if you are integrating the work of several researchers.

Estimate YOUR time for editing, revising, and "producing" the report

The tendency is to allow too little time for writing a first draft.

Allow enough time to complete the writing **properly**. This point was noted repeatedly by both researchers and managers in our survey. One researcher put it this way:

> "I think the time required to produce quality writing is severely underestimated by management. Getting started is hard when there's no guarantee enough time will be allowed to finish..."

Another claimed, and several managers agreed:

> "Good writing takes time, lots of it. We all underestimate how long it will take. [Yet] sloppy writing leaves the impression that the research was sloppy."

Time for revising and producing the report, including the hours for those helping you, must be part of your schedule.

After you've estimated and planned your time for writing the first draft, allow yourself at least half that time again to go over the report and edit for content. Then, according to how much outside assistance you are planning, calculate how much additional time you'll need for language editing, formatting, and production stages of the report.

Estimate the time for non-author work

When you ask a colleague for a technical review, or call in others for assistance in word processing, editing, designing, proofreading, or printing, find out how much time they will need.

1st Revised outline for B-TIP report on
NDT TECHNOLOGY: ADVANCES AND APPLICATIONS

No. of pages, double spaced

I PROBLEM <u>Why companies need to use NDT</u>
* Definition of NDT *
* Uses: technical reasons and business incentives
* Used by: Airforce, railroads, auto industry (others) + examples — 6-8
* Benefits companies have gained

II SCOPE * Overview of current + emerging technologies and business implications and evaluations. — 1

III SOLUTION <u>NDT technologies</u>
* Basic principles of wave interaction with matter (General) — 5
* Primary Technologies: (Specific)
- Eddy current — 4
- Magnetic particle — 4
- Ultrasonic, including acoustic emission, acoustic analysis, vibration — 4
- Radiography, including neutron radiography — 4
- Liquid penetrant — 4

For each primary technology, discuss:
- How it works } Tech
- How it is implemented }
- Advantages and disadvantages Tech + Bus
- Uses, both current and potential – Bus.
- State of the art, and future developments Tech + Bus

* Secondary, SPECIALIZED technologies
- Thermal, IR, internal dusting
- Optical, laser — 1
- Visual
- Optical holographic
- Microwave

Information for these technologies to be presented in a table:

Method	Operating principle	Character. detected	Main use	Advant.	Limit.	Potential use & development	Comments
	Tech		Bus	Tech + Bus		Bus + Tech	Bus + Tech

* Emerging technologies
- Synthetic aperture focusing
- Tomographic reconstruction methods — 1-2

\+ -Discuss: new capabilities, how it works, date available, cost – Tech + Bus. — 1-2

IMPLEMENTATION <u>Selecting ~~an~~ + integrating an NDT system</u>
* Steps to go through -- Tech — 3
* Specification of problem: company needs, date, reliability needs, cost limits Tech + Bus. — 3
* Integrating a system into the production line Tech — 2
* Data management Tech — 2

IV RESULTS * Potential problems, benefits and risks for management Bus + Tech — 4

V CONCLUSION <u>Outlook for NDT and its use</u>
* Technical outlook - developments foreseen
* Application outlook -- barriers and incentives Bus + Tech
* Economics - price trends Bus. — 6-8
* Market trends Bus.
* Business opportunities Bus.
* Scenario Bus + Tech

* Non-Destructive Testing

Total pages 55-61

Note how the outline, though not yet complete, already follows the double-5 organizational scheme, with the number of pages assigned to the items of each part. Note also how each section includes both technical and business information.

Here's the basic time division we use for planning a B-TIP report.

As an example of breaking out time and tasks, here are some insights into how we plan a B-TIP report. We use the following time-division scheme to help researcher-authors plan their time and integrate their work with reviewers, editors, and designers.

Time divisions for B-TIP reports

Author time, percent	Work stage	Researcher's tasks	Help after researcher's task is completed
15	Outline	Prepare outline	Editorial and technical review for **content**, organization, and level of detail; often done in brainstorming sessions
35	1st draft	Write	Editorial and technical review to assure inclusion of needed information for B-TIP members; questions and suggestions to researcher to improve content
18	2nd draft	Review 1st draft for content; respond to reviewers' questions	Edit by B-TIP staff for clarity, organization, consistency, logic, style, graphics; discussions with author to clarify questions
14	3rd draft	Review and fine tune edited 2nd draft	Final check by B-TIP editors
18	Production	Review text, tables, and diagrams at critical points to assure accuracy	B-TIP editorial staff work with designers and use publishing software to produce final document

You can adapt this concept to allocate time on a major report or proposal:

▶

Though you may not need the same level of outside attention for all your documents, this model can be adapted for your usual writing tasks. You can plan on less time for "production" and more time for the original draft. An adapted version of the percentage-time division for a researcher's input to a large proposal or report might be:

Author time, percent	Work Stage	Adaptations
15	Outline	Researcher can also use some of this time to review the outline with the manager and to plan the writing schedule. This process may take a few iterations.
40	1st draft	Researcher can reserve 5 percent of this time for technical and editorial reviews of content
20	2nd draft	Researcher reviews and revises content; integrates reviewers' suggestions
15	3rd draft	Researcher reviews and edits the document for style, clarity, consistency
10	Production	Researcher reviews layout, including text, figures, and tables, and proofreads final printout.

Now, let's look at the amount of the total time requirements that researchers can delegate to others:

- 3 to 5 percent for the outline: an editor can help plan the document, work procedure, and schedule.

- 5 percent for the first draft: reviewers can give constructive suggestions.

- 5 to 15 percent for the 2nd draft: an editor can help assure useful organization, logic, and completeness from the readers' view and can help integrate reviewers' suggestions.

- 12 percent for the 3rd draft: a competent editor can probably do these tasks better than the researcher; the researcher would clarify the editor's questions and review the end product.

- 8 percent for the final production time: others can do most of the proofreading, final checking, and corrections.

Thus, researchers could save some 33 to 45 percent of the time they often spend on a writing job!

...reducing the time a researcher spends by up to 45 percent.

Prepare a detailed schedule based on the inputs of all the participants

In addition to hourly estimates for each task, the researcher and other participants will need to provide "dates" when they will be available for this writing project. With such information, the researcher can work out a detailed, realistic schedule for completing the publication.

However, for large, multi-authored documents, a "champion" with enough clout and tact—whether the editor, researcher, or manager—must be assigned the task of making sure that all the participants contribute their inputs on time.

Each of these suggestions can help you make a dent in the time problem. Although we've devoted a lot of space to a realistic scheduling procedure, implementing it doesn't take much additional planning time. But the gains in quality and productivity (let alone the savings in anxiety) are worth the effort.

Careful scheduling along these lines will increase productivity—and quality.

If you arrive at a time estimate your manager cannot agree to, or if your time estimate does not meet a preset deadline, you can try one of the alternatives to shorten or streamline the writing tasks, as described on pages 82 and 83.

Style: Language and format*

Now, let's turn our attention to **language and format**, collectively called **"style"**. We'll start with a key barrier for many readers: understanding researchers' language.

Both researchers and managers named the **"long convoluted sentence"** as the main problem that impeded readers' understanding. Next, managers listed the use of **jargon** and problems in **word choice**. Finally, they were concerned with difficulty in **quickly grasping** the writer's intent.

By far, the three major language problems are sentence length, word choice and jargon. They prevent rapid comprehension.

What can researchers do to remedy these problems? Let's look at these difficulties one by one.

---

* We have combined the main problems of the "style" and "mechanics" survey questions in this section. We've called it "Style" because these elements are more stylistic than mechanical.

Avoiding—and fixing—the long, convoluted sentence

The most common causes of long, convoluted sentences are:

A review of researchers' drafts[*] narrows this problem to the nine most common language pitfalls:

▶

- Overusing the word "and"
- Handling pronouns imprecisely
- Clinging to the passive voice
- Using too many prepositions
- Relying on "clutter" words and "crutch" phrases
- Repeating expressions
- Adding unnecessary adjectives and adverbs
- Hedging too much
- Constructing sentences with more than 30 words

Now, spend a little time reading the "rules";
then review the examples
—extracted from actual reports—
and corrections.

We believe that if researchers pay attention to these elements alone, the clarity and readability of their writing will improve immensely. To demonstrate these flaws, we'll use sentences collected from actual reports. Unfortunately, many of these sentences illustrate more than one failing! But they're real examples, not sentences concocted just to prove a point.[**]

Here's what you can try to do.

Use "and" sparingly

Overusing "and" causes an amazing number of poor sentences. The reason: "and" is so pervasive. It connects sentences, clauses, and phrases; it connects lists of words and bulleted items; and it mandates parallelism.

"And" presents two pitfalls: first, overuse can lead to long, "run-on" sentences...

To use "and" successfully, just remember a few suggestions and warnings. We cover them in two major categories.

- "And" can make sentences very long
- Items connected by "and" must be parallel.

1. **"And" can make sentences very long. And** it is very tempting to use—because you often don't want to go back **and** repeat the introductory part of another sentence, **and** so you just tack on an "and" **and** continue ... **and** before you know it you've completed a whole paragraph **and** you haven't wasted a single period.

that tire and confuse the reader.

These unrelated "tack-ons" form a "run-on sentence" of piled-up ideas that confuse the reader.

You can use three solutions to end the "and" problem:

Here are three solutions:

▶

- Break the long sentence into two or more smaller sentences.
- Use other connectives.
- Recast the sentence.

---

[*] We reviewed about 30 drafts of B-TIP reports from the years 1980–1985.

[**] To gain maximum benefit from this section, cover the correction; then see how you would improve the original sentence!

Sometimes you'll need to use all these techniques to "fix" one sentence.

Here are some **examples** of misused "ands"...and **corrections**. We'll highlight the "bad ands" in each example.

Example	Comment	Correction
"For PAS in the infrared region, conventional infrared spectrometers can be utilized **and** thus the only expense (if a spectrometer is available) is the cost of the construction of the PAS cell and the associated optics necessary to couple the PAS cell **and** the spectrometer."	To get a better version, divide the sentence into two; then use "with" to replace "and".	For PAS in the infrared region, conventional infrared spectrometers can be used. Thus, if a spectrometer is available, the only expense is the cost of constructing the PAS cell and the optics needed to couple the cell **with** the spectrometer.

Here's another example:

Example	Comment	Correction
"For the new drug entity, complete preclinical and clinical trials are required to gain approval **and** often post-approval surveillance is undertaken."	To improve this sentence, break it into two sentences; then recast the first sentence.	Approval of a new drug requires satisfactory results from complete pre-clinical and clinical trials. Often, post-approval surveillance is undertaken as well.

Look at this one:

Example	Comment	Correction
"The solvent ion-exchange process makes possible reduction of waste tailings **and** also eliminates the classic recovery of copper from dilute solution by scrap iron **and** the subsequent pyrometallurgical processing with attendant air pollution and slag dumps."	To obtain a shorter, clearer description, break the sentence into three; then recast the first and third sentences.	Use of the solvent ion exchange process reduces waste tailings. It also eliminates the classic recovery of copper from dilute solution by scrap iron. In addition, it eliminates the pyrometallurgical processing that results in air pollution and slag dumps.

2. **Items connected by "and" must be PARALLEL**. This key concept, dealt with in detail in many textbooks on style, emerges as a huge stumbling block for many researchers.

Second, "and" is too often used to connect non-parallel concepts or structures.

The concept may be easier to understand if you look at words as if they were numbers. Just as you can't add different types of numbers without putting them into a **similar form**—e.g., you can't add two or more fractions without finding a common denominator—so, to use language correctly, you can't (or at least shouldn't!) "add" or combine words, phrases, or clauses in a sentence without putting them into a **similar form**.

"Similar form" essentially means using the same structural or grammatical form for all parts of the series. To explain, we'll use some elementary grammatical terms. For example:

"To build this piece of equipment you will need **nuts, bolts, and screws**."—a series of nouns.

"The book was widely read **by researchers in many companies and by teachers in many universities**."—two similarly constructed prepositional phrases.

"We expect **that this experiment will achieve its goals and that it will open new market vistas**."—two similarly constructed clauses: both start with "that", both use the future tense, and both have direct objects.

Now, let's look at some examples of non-parallel construction, describe where they went wrong, and see how to improve them.

Example	Comment	Correction
"The pulsed mode of (laser) operation **leaves** the adjacent material virtually unaffected **and** no chips or burns **are left** as is common with conventional drilling".	In this sentence, the **verbs** in the two clauses are not parallel: one is active, the other is passive. A better construction would be:	The pulsed mode of operation **leaves** the adjacent material virtually unaffected **and eliminates** the chips or burrs that are common with conventional drilling.

Look at this example:

Example	Comment	Correction
"Because of its unique adsorption properties, activated carbon will find increasing use **in pollution control and simultaneously recovering** materials for reuse."	Here, the two **phrases following "in"** are not parallel. One solution would be:	Because of its unique adsorption properties, activated carbon will find increasing use **in controlling** pollution **and**, simultaneously, **in recovering** materials for reuse.

Watch for lack of parallel construction in many of the other examples we show. You'll see how prevalent it is!

Use pronouns precisely

Correctly used, pronouns can reduce the number of words needed to express an idea. They are shorthand forms that enable us to refer to previous concepts—words, phrases, sentences, or even whole paragraphs and sections. These pronouns include words used as:

- Subjects (I, you, he, she, we, they, one, it)
- Objects (me, her, him, us, them, one, it)
- Possessives (mine, ours, his, hers, yours, theirs, one's its)
- Relative pronouns (who, which, that)
- Demonstratives (this, that, these, those)

Pronouns cause problems when the item they refer to is unclear or unidentified,

A problem arises, particularly in English[*], when the item the pronoun refers to is unclear. Another difficulty arises from giving the same pronoun two different connotations within the same sentence. A third problem—widely encountered but

[*] Several other languages have differences in word gender that help clarify pronoun references.

often excused—is the "dangling" or unidentified "demonstrative". Again, here are some typical misuses—and suggestions for correcting them. First, an example of a double connotation for the pronoun "it".

when they have different connotations in the same sentence,

and when they dangle.

Example	Comment	Correction
"This duration of release would be of great value since, once a wound is self-contained, **it** is difficult to get antibiotics into **it**."	To get rid of the double connotation, you can eliminate the "it is difficult"—a poor construction anyway. You could write instead:	This release duration would be exceedingly valuable because antibiotics are difficult to introduce into the wound after **it** becomes self contained.

Or, look at this triple use of it!

"**It** is estimated that **it** took five thousand dollars above budget to complete **it**."	Why not say:	The completed project cost an estimated $5000 over budget.

A dangling "this, without an accompanying noun, can cause ambiguity:

"Because of **this**, FT-IR techniques will be..." "**This** shows that..."	We never know clearly whether "this" stands for: the above reason? a particular experiment shows? or a previously described incident shows? To correct such sentences, define the "this":	For **this reason**, FT-IR techniques... **This experiment** shows that...

Sometimes great bloopers can emerge from unclearly referenced pronouns.

"The problem of long-term responsibility for off-site disposal of **one's** hazardous wastes is another cost item which currently is still difficult to estimate."	Surely the author was referring to the **company's** hazardous waste...	

Strongly prefer the active voice

Constantly using the passive voice lengthens sentences, convolutes meaning, and obscures accountability. Yet, in the name of "objectivity", the passive voice has become a hallmark of so-called "scientific" writing.

For example, why complicate a sentence by writing:

> "The report was given to the manager by the researchers." (10 words)

when you can simply say:

> "The researchers gave the manager the report." (7 words)

Another example:

> "It was estimated that the project would cost $2,000,000."

Such phrasing begs the question, "WHO estimated?". We need to define this unknown "it"—perhaps the project team? X? X and Y? the accounting department?...

Even worse are the "padded passives" that add bulk but no meaning to a sentence. Typical "padding" taps such words as achieved, accomplished, used, conducted, attained, performed. Here are some examples.

"Production of optical fibers **can be achieved** by our company by..." (11 words)

(Notice how easily we could substitute "accomplished", "performed" or "attained" for "achieved"!)

Even a "normal passive" is shorter:

"Optical fibers **can be produced** by our company by..." (9 words)

Better still, we can "actively" write:

"Our company **can produce** optical fibers by..." (7 words)

Clearly, using the active voice simplifies—"de-convolutes"—the sentence. Check the overly long sentences on pages 63 to 65 for further proof.

Reduce preposition use

Prepositions—one of the worst banes of the non-native speaker of any language[*]—can also impede the readers' grasp. Because prepositions signal **changes** in direction (toward, from, to), ownership (of), time (before, after), or place (above, below), their frequent use convolutes sentences...and tires readers.

Count the prepositions in both versions of the upcoming examples; the numbers prove the importance of reducing preposition use to simplify sentences and communicate directly. Notice how reducing preposition use also shortens the sentence.

One major way to decrease preposition use is to convert nouns into verb forms.

To reduce the number of prepositions—which impede communication when overused—you can often convert nouns into verb forms...

Example	Comment	Correction
"Because **of** this, chemiluminescence techniques will be **of** vital and increasing importance **to** the **accurate evaluation of** autoxidative service life **of** organic materials". (5 prepositions and a dangling "this")	We could write instead:	**For** this reason, chemiluminescence techniques will be vitally important **for accurately evaluating** autoxidative service life **of** organic materials. (3 prepositions) (We did not eliminate the final preposition because the long modifier string—"organic materials' autoxidative service life"—is even more deadly!)

Another way to reduce the number of prepositions is to convert nouns to adjectives or adverbs (as we did in the above sentence: "importance" became "important"), and adjectives to adverbs. Sometimes we need to use both techniques in the same sentence. Thus in the next example, "'close control of" becomes "'closely control". Also, we can change prepositional phrases to single words (e.g., replace "'to a higher degree" with "greater").

convert nouns to adjectives or adverbs, or convert adjectives to adverbs.

Example	Comment	Correction
"**Close control of** the composition **in the** column product and feed **by** using gas chromatography can assure that the products are recovered **from** the residue **to a higher degree**." (5 prepositions)	A smoother version with fewer prepositions would read:	But, using gas chromatography **to closely control** column product and feed composition can assure **greater** product recovery **from** the residue. (2 prepositions)

---

[*] Although this section specifically deals with smoothing out these problems in English, the concept may be applicable to other languages as well.

Here is another example:

| "The advantages **to** the utilization **of** mono-clonal antibodies **in** drug delivery systems is the targeting **of** drugs **to** specific tissues or sites **in** the body **through** antigen-antibody interactions." (7 prepositions) | Monoclonal antibodies can advantageously deliver drugs **to** specific tissues or sites **through** antigen-antibody interactions. (2 prepositions) |

Several other commonly used prepositional phrases or forms can be stream-lined. For example:

was lower **in** cost	= cost less
was **of** greater importance	= was more important
in regard **to**	= regarding
in order **to**	= to
in that	= because
associated **with**	= for
the writing **of** papers	= writing papers
the targeting **of** drugs	= targeting drugs
are **of** importance	= are important
to be used **in** place **of**	= to replace
in terms **of**	= by or for

Avoid "clutter" words and "crutch" phrases

Many languages have "clutter" and "crutch" words and phrases that make it easy to form sentences—but add bulk. Unfortunately, "scientific" writers store a large group of "crutch" phrases in their arsenals. Such words impede the reader's grasp of the subject especially if the content is already difficult. We call them "watch-out words". When you see them in your own work, try to find better alternatives.

Some well-worn words and phrases—"clutter words and crutch phrases"—may help the writer, but not the reader.

Typical clutter and crutch phrases to flag:

- there are
- there being no or (some)
- it is ... apparent that
    - ... important to note that
    - ... interesting to consider that
    - ... of interest that
- in such a manner as to
- in a fashion such that
- in the presence of
- some means of
- is such that
- the phenomenon of
- it is believed that ... (Notice that in this passive "crutch" phrase and the next four, the writer not only clutters the sentence but evades responsibility! Identify **who** "believes", "estimates", "discovered", "feels", or "sees".)
    - ... it is estimated that
    - ... it has recently been discovered
    - ... it is generally felt that
    - ... it can be seen that
- has the potential of.

Here are some examples of "clutter and crutch" usage—and improvements. Notice how removing the bulk added by the clutter and crutch words has slimmed down the sentence. Note also that many passive verbs have been "activated"—a point we discuss on pages 57 and 68. These words and phrases often go hand in hand with passive construction.

Example	Correction
"In the past twenty years, **there has been** a growing interest in the **phenomenon of** substantial solubility of organic compounds in supercritical solvents."	In the past 20 years, interest in enhanced solubility of organic compounds in supercritical solvents has grown.
"Mass spectrometry **is such that** while a high level of training and experience is needed to align and maintain the mass spectrometer,..."	Although alignment and maintenance of mass spectrometers require highly trained and experienced operators,...
"The critical range **is such as to allow...**"	The critical range **allows...**
"The technique **has the potential of** reducing recycle time..."	The technique **could** reduce recycle time...
"**Due to their potential in causing** water pollution..."	**Because** they **could** pollute water resources...
"**It has recently been** discovered..."	**Researchers at Caltech** recently discovered...
"**It is believed** that	**We** believe...; or, **Many researchers** believe...
"**It is estimated** that..."	**Our research team** estimates that..
"Ignoring this issue can result in a project management system for each of the pieces with **there being no accountability** or management for the delivery of the integrated product."	Ignoring this issue can result in a project management system for each of the pieces **without accountability** for delivering the integrated product.

Eliminate repetitive expressions

Repetition makes sentences unduly long. To revise sentences, first highlight the repetitive words or phrases. (Here we've set them in boldface.) Then try to delete them, or to reconstruct the sentence; sometimes, both. For example:

Various forms of repetition can lengthen sentences and impede reading.

Example	Comment	Correction
"In some instances, microencapsulated pesticides presented a **special and specific** hazard to bees."	What the researcher really meant was:	In one case, a microencapsulated pesticide proved hazardous to bees.
"There will be advances in the production of **human antibodies** or isolation of **human antibodies** in their use in drug delivery instead of animal derived antibodies so that the immune reactions are not present."		Advances in producing or isolating **human antibodies** to replace animal-derived antibodies in drug delivery systems will eliminate immune reactions.
"Three important features of PAS make this method unique. ■ **There first is the fact that...** ■ **The second feature of PAS** is its ability to... ■ **The third unique feature of PAS is the fact that** the method requires no sample preparation."	A frequent, space-consuming mistake... but easily corrected:	Three important features of PAS make it unique. PAS: ■ Does A ■ Can do B ■ Requires no sample preparation
"These detectors have been used **for the direct determination of** aromatic hydrocarbons in gasoline and jet fuels and **for the determination of** rotenone in fish extracts."		These instruments have been used to **detect** aromatic hydrocarbons in gasoline and jet fuels, and rotenone in fish extracts.
"With the automation currently existing in **gas chromatography**, both in sampling and data handling, it is relatively easy to train and utilize inexperienced personnel for operating **gas chromatographs**."	Why not shorten this sentence to:	With present automation of sampling and data handling, a company can easily train inexperienced personnel to operate **gas chromatographs.**
"Another current **limitation** on **microcapsules** is their nonsuitability for intravenous administration. This is a **limitation** if a circulating **microcapsule** loaded with drug is desired for any **long length** of time."	We can remove the repetitions by writing:	Another **limitation** on microcapsules is their unsuitability for intravenous administration where circulation is desired for any **extended** period.

Avoid excessive adjectives and adverbs

Some researchers feel that, in the name of accuracy or emphasis, they must qualify almost everything they write. They plunk in adjectives and adverbs freely.

But, unnecessary adjectives clutter and confuse the reader's grasp; they also demand extra reading time.

To correct this problem, delete the "offenders". Or, scrap the sentence and start from scratch.

Adjectives and adverbs are useful—but you don't have to qualify everything!

Thus, instead of:

Example	Comment	Correction
"It's **extremely** important that this **highly sensitive** test be interpreted **correctly** by **highly trained** scientists, not by **low-level** technicians."	We can write—and readers will understand far better:	Results of this **difficult** test should be interpreted by **experienced** scientists.

Here's another example.

Example	Comment	Correction
"Since the **autoxidation degradation** of organic materials is **virtually a universal** occurrence, chemiluminescence from organic materials is **similarly** an **almost universally observed** phenomenon."		Since all organic materials degrade by autoxidation, chemiluminescence from organic materials is **almost universally** observed.

Also, don't modify absolutes. "Unique", for example, means one of a kind. Something can't be "very" unique, or "more" unique.

Don't over-hedge

Along the same line, hedging is too often carried to extremes.

The need to qualify is carried even further when, in the name of scientific exactness, researchers add caveat upon caveat to hedge their statements. (Though our first example is an exaggeration, it is not atypical!).

Example	Comment	Correction
From our work so far, **it would seem** that the **likelihood** of this event happening has not **yet** been **sufficiently** proven for **tentative** conclusions to be drawn.	A quintuple hedge! We can write—and readers will understand far better:	From our work **so far**, we can't draw conclusions about this event.
	If that statement is too strong, add one more hedge:	From our work **so far**, we haven't **yet** reached conclusions about this event

But here are some actual examples:

Example	Comment	Correction
"Gelatin capsules, even after hardening treatments, are **frequently** difficult to process in order to obtain a free flowing dry powder product. **When** this is an **essential** requirement for a **specific** use, it will **probably be necessary** to use **fairly** complex drying systems."	Couldn't we get by with:	Even after hardening treatments, gelatin capsules **often** do not yield a free-flowing dry powder. To obtain such products, complex drying systems **may** be needed. (A double instead of sextuple hedge.)

Or:

"It is **occasionally possible** to prevent agglomeration by spray drying the capsules slurry at **some selected stage** after the capsule wall has formed."	The reader will understand better if you just say:	Agglomeration can **sometimes** be prevented by spray drying the capsular slurry after the capsule wall has formed.

As you go through your draft, fearlessly remove all these kinds of clutter. One technique for training yourself in this craft is illustrated in "Plain English for Lawyers"(!)[6]: review a sentence, circle the essential words, look at what's left...and see what you can throw out.

Or, try the opposite approach. Review a sentence for crutches, hedges, descriptors, and prepositions. Delete them if possible; or convert them to simpler forms. If these steps aren't enough, reconstruct the sentence.

Cut back sentence length

Journalism schools teach budding reporters that sentences should not exceed 20 words. But, for researchers, we'll up that number by 50 percent to 30 words. This tip doesn't mean you should never a write a sentence with more than 30 words. It means most of your sentences should be far less than 30 words.

Long sentences—those with more than 30 words—usually hinder communications; try to shorten or divide them.

To revise overly long sentences, first delete extraneous words. Use all the tools we've discussed. Then, if necessary, divide the remainder into two or three sentences. For example:

Example	Edit	Correction
"Because of the extreme sensitivity of chemiluminescence techniques, chemiluminescence-based approaches to the evaluation of autoxidation and degradation of organic materials can often be applied to materials which are only subtly changed by oxidative degradation." Here's what we could do:	Because ~~of the~~ extreme*ly* sensiti~~vity of,~~ *they are* *e* chemiluminescence technique*s* *can often be used* ~~chemiluminescence-based approaches~~ to ~~the~~ evalua*te* ~~of~~ autoxidation and degradation of organic materials ~~can e~~ ~~often be applied to materials which~~ *that* are only subtly change*d* ~~by oxidative~~ ~~degradation.~~	Thus, here's our corrected version: Because they are extremely sensitive, chemiluminescence techniques can often be used to evaluate autoxidation and degradation of organic materials that are only subtly changed.

Example	Edit	Correction

''Suitable adhesive formulations, based on resin capsules and a stannic chloride catalyst, possessed good shelf life, and when they were used in such a way that adequate mixing occurred, bond strengths were obtained comparable to, although somewhat lower than, those of conventional liquid epoxy adhesives.

Edit column (handwritten edits shown):

Some ~~Suitable~~ adhesive formulations, based on resin capsules and a stannic chloride catalyst, ~~possessed~~ have already shown good shelf life, and ~~when they were used in such a way that~~ adequate ~~mixing occurred, bond strengths were obtained comparable to, although somewhat lower than, those of conventional liquid epoxy adhesives.~~

Correction column:

Thus, we would write—and the reader would get the idea better:

Some adhesive formulations, based on resin capsules and a stannic chloride catalyst, have already shown good shelf life and adequate bond strength.

Now, look at this beauty:

''Economic considerations involving the implementation of process modifications dictate that these result in increased process efficiency, an actual profit, or at least an avoidance of a treatment and/or a disposal cost, which dictates that the capital cost not be excessive and that an economically viable scale of operation can be achieved.'' (one sentence with 51 words)

Yes—it's for real! But how about this revision:

Edit column (handwritten edits shown):

Economic considerations ~~involving the~~ dictate ~~implementation of~~ process modifications ~~dictate that these result in~~ increased that generate process efficiency, an actual profit, or at least ~~an avoidance of a~~ treatment and/or a disposal cost, ~~which dictates~~ These factors also mandate reasonable ~~that the~~ capital cost ~~not be excessive~~ and ~~that~~ an economically viable scale of operation ~~can be achieved.~~

Correction column:

Economic considerations dictate that process modifications increase process efficiency, generate an actual profit, or at least avoid treatment or disposal costs. These factors also mandate reasonable capital costs and an economically viable scale of operation.

(2 sentences of 21 and 14 words, total 35 words)

Example	Edit	Correction
"Once promising opportunities for process modifications have been identified, obtain bids from several equipment manufacturers (or on-site or off-site equipment modifiers) and several process or materials suppliers (if specific processes or materials are involved) giving costs and timeframes involved, so that one can use these data in making final decisions regarding the desirability of carrying out process modifications on selected operations." (62 words in one sentence!)	*After identifying* Once promising opportunities for process modifications, ~~have been identified,~~ *time and cost* obtain bids from several equipment manufacturers ~~(or on-site~~ or ~~off-site equipment~~ modifiers)~~,~~ and *from* several process or materials suppliers. ~~(if specific processes or materials are involved) giving costs and timeframes involved, so that one can use these~~ data. *Using the bid* ~~in making final~~ *de which,* decisions regarding the *if any,* ~~desirability of carrying out~~ process*es to* *to* modifications ~~on selected operations.~~	After identifying promising opportunities for process modifications, obtain time and cost bids from several equipment manufacturers or modifiers, and from several process or materials suppliers. Using the bid data, decide which, if any, processes to modify. (2 sentences of 25 and 10 words; 35 total)

But here's our champion ...

"Success will not be achieved against the goals of implementing the Project Management System without an environment of belief on the part of all involved of the benefits to the corporate entity and the individual from the system's use and acceptance on the part of all involved of the impact of implementing the Project Management System on both institution methods and individual behavior." (63 words) Note: • the number of prepositions • the number of ands • the number of nouns.	*A Project Management System,* ~~Success will not be achieved against~~ *succeed* ~~the goals of implementing the Project~~ *unless* ~~Management System without an en-~~ ~~vironment of belief on the part of all in-~~ *the participants believe the company will* ~~volved of the benefits to the corporate~~ ~~entity and the individual from the~~ *They must also,* ~~system's use and~~ acceptance ~~on the~~ *system's* ~~part of all involved of the~~ impact ~~of im-~~ ~~plementing the Project Management~~ *business procedures* ~~System on both institution methods~~ *' responsibilities,* and individual ~~behavior.~~	Here's the easier-to-grasp alternative: A Project Management System will not succeed unless all the participants believe the company will benefit. They must also accept the system's impact on business procedures and individuals' responsibilities. (2 sentences of 16 and 13 words; 29 total)

By integrating these suggestions into your language habits, you will simplify and shorten the sentences you write. Your writing will also be clearer and more readable.[*]

But above all, make sure your sentences make sense. Don't get caught with something like:

Example	Comment	Correction
"In all, there are probably 25-30 such assays which have left some confusion as to just which ones to use and how to interpret immunological effects."	Surely the assays aren't confused! But the assay users might be. . . .	Because some 25 to 30 such assays are available, researchers are uncertain which ones to use and are unsure how to interpret immunological effects.

Choosing the right words and handling jargon

Here are some suggestions on word choice:

While researchers in our survey worried about finding the right words, especially to explain complex technical work, managers complained about an overabundance of jargon.

Here are some suggestions that have worked for us.

Use ordinary words

• Use ordinary words—don't struggle to find a fancy word when the plain one delivers your message.

Especially in your first draft, don't be afraid to use plain words to express your thoughts. For example:

> "This simplified technique still makes it possible to get pretty good answers, but saves us a lot of time."

If you want to improve the sentence later, you can. Don't waste time at the first draft stage (and even later) over "makes it possible" (though you could say "enables us"): later you might want to change "pretty good" to "adequate" or "good enough". Or you might switch the sentence around and end up with:

> This simplified technique saves us time but still gives us adequate results.

A good sentence with ordinary words.

Find the right word

• But, do find the right word—that is, the most accurate word.

Suppose you're just not satisfied with the word choice. What can you do?

■ **Use a thesaurus**. Interestingly, you may find you're looking for a better word under the wrong category. Sometimes synonyms in the thesaurus will lead you to a different, more fruitful trail.

■ **Ask an editor or a reviewer**. If your company has a "hotline" to an editorial consultant, call and ask. If colleagues or managers are reviewing your document,

---

[*] For texts on "Style", see the bibliography, page 168.

circle the word and ask if they can suggest a more precise alternative. But be sure you're looking for a more accurate word, not just a fancier word.

Make a note of good words during your reading

When you read well written articles in your field, (e.g., in *Scientific American, Science,* or some other journal), try to spot the words—particularly the verbs—that add precision and shorten the sentence. If you can, make more than a mental note: keep a small list of "Key words I may need".

• *In your reading, note words that add precision—then put them in your word bank.*

Use transition words

Transition words—such as: because, when, while, thus, however, but, despite, although, conversely—**guide the reader to your precise intent.**

For example, instead of using "and" to construct a vague sentence, insert an exact transition word:

• *Use transition words that add direction or logic.*

Example	Comment	Correction
"The technicians' work in the lab was intense **and** it was decided they had to do overtime."	Does "and" mean "because"? when? whenever? yet? Clarify.	**Because** so much work piled up in the lab, the technicians had to work overtime.

Such words improve the flow from thought to thought. But even more important: by showing cause and effect, or other logical relations, they provide "cues" that help readers follow your reasoning or assessment. Use transition words liberally—within and between sentences, between paragraphs, even between document sections.

Use action VERBS

Using a dull noun plus "is," "occurred," or "accomplished" takes extra space and makes heavy reading. Ditto for passive verbs. Instead, try converting the noun to a verb; a passive to an active verb.

- *Active, action verbs usually lighten a reader's chore.*

For example:

Example	Correction
"The water **vaporization was accomplished** by the sun.""	**The sun vaporized** the water.
"These results **are seen** in the growing trend..."	These results **reflect** a growing trend...
"This tendency **was given** impetus..."	This tendency **gained** impetus...
"This may result in GaAs cells **being competitive** in cost with silicon devices."	Thus, GaAs cells **may compete** in cost with silicon devices.

Use jargon judiciously

- *While jargon should be avoided when possible, it is often necessary.*

Jargon, the readers' bane, is the researchers' joy. In truth, jargon is almost inevitable: it emerges from the researcher's need for a shorthand to express new concepts or to compress a multi-word expression into a single word or acronym. Often, what starts as "jargon" becomes an accepted, widely used part of the language. For example, former computer "lingo" words—like input, output, RAM, K's of memory, software—are now common vocabulary.

But jargon must be used with extreme care; otherwise the reader, who may even be a researcher in a related field, will not understand:

"The fundamental modulation mechanism for birefringent polarization modulators is differential phase modulation induced on orthogonally polarized components of the optical wave."

Also, researchers need to be careful about the words they press into action to represent new concepts. For example:

"Such sensor tips could consist of Fabry-Perot cavities, photoelastic polarization, optical levers, or **frustrated** internal reflection devices."

I DON'T KNOW WHO'S MORE FRUSTRATED— ME...OR THAT INTERNAL REFLECTION DEVICE !!

So, when some jargon is vital to a discussion, what can you do?

But, when technical terms must be used:

■ First and foremost, recognize that most readers will not understand some terms you use. Don't assume that "everyone" knows what GC/MS or CIMS stand for or that "everyone" knows what liposomes are.

■ Try to keep highly technical terms to a minimum. Check carefully if you **must** use a specific term. Maybe you can substitute an easier-to-understand, explanatory phrase.

■ Define technical terms and all acronyms you use. If you're not sure whether or not to define a term, define it.

■ If you need only a few "relatively easy" terms, define them in parentheses right after you use them (i.e., _____).

■ If you need to use many terms and acronyms, make a list or glossary for the reader. For example, many of our reports include a glossary of terms near the beginning. (See example on page 70.[7])

■ Be **consistent**; use the same technical term to mean the same thing throughout your document. Sometimes you may be tempted to substitute a different term for sake of "variety". Sometimes different researchers use different terms to denote the same meaning. Or occasionally they use the same term for two different concepts. This confusion of terms unduly burdens even the empathetic reader.

The other side of the coin is equally important: managers must **expect to learn** new concepts and terms to keep up-to-date on the research they support. As one researcher commented in our questionnaire: "How about writing a report on 'Helping Managers Understand What researchers Write'!"

Minimize grammatical, punctuation, and spelling errors

Avoid errors in usage; enlist proofreading help.

Though we deliberately have not stressed these "mechanical" language problems in this book, such easily recognized mistakes can indeed irritate readers and impede their comprehension. To avoid outright spelling errors, routinely use the "spellcheckers" included in many word processing packages. However, spellcheckers are not foolproof; for example, they **cannot** detect correct word use ("here" or "hear"; "steel" or "steal"). Software that spots grammar and punctuation errors (e.g., "Grammatik" and "Rightwriter") may also be useful as a first pass— but are also not yet perfectly foolproof, comprehensive, or relevant to technical writing. A long-time favorite guide for correct usage is the book, "Elements of Style" by Strunk and White (see Bibliography for details). But only thorough proofreading can catch all errors. After going through several drafts of a document, you're not apt to be a proficient "proofer". Ask someone for help; an editor or peer is best.

GLOSSARY

Many terms used in this Review may not be familiar to those who are not metallurgists. This glossary will help.

coercive force—The demagnetizing force needed to remove the residual magnetism of a metal or alloy.

core loss—The energy loss in transformers due to eddy currents and magnetostriction. This energy loss is usually dissipated in the form of heat.

domains—Zones within a magnetic material in which all the magnetic moments are aligned in the same direction.

domain wall—Regions between domains, about 50 atoms thick, where the magnetic moments change directions rather abruptly. Movement of domain walls is resisted by grain boundaries or microstructural defects.

enthalpy—The heat content of a material as determined by its heat capacity and the absolute temperature.

eutectic—The composition at which an alloy has its lowest melting point.

free energy—The total energy content of a material. At a given temperature, a material is at equilibrium when the free energy is at its lowest possible value.

hysteresis loop—A closed figure formed by plotting magnetizing force against flux density for a magnetic material. To complete one loop the magnetizing force is taken through a cycle of increasing and decreasing values.

magnetostriction—The change in dimensions produced when a magnetic material is placed in a magnetic field.

metalloid—An element having both metallic and non-metallic properties.

metastable—A material state at which the material becomes unstable with any infinitesimal change.

remanence—The residual magnetism of a ferromagnetic substance that has been subjected to a hysteresis cycle, when the magnetizing force has been reduced to zero.

segregation—The non-uniform distribution or concentration of impurities or alloying constituents that can arise during solidification.

spinoidal decomposition—The precipitation of a second phase by compositional fluctuations (diffusion controlled) that oppose the normal composition gradient, i.e., solute moves to an already solute rich region present in the solid at ambient temperature.

supersaturation—A metastable solution or alloy containing an amount of alloying element exceeding the equilibrium amount at that temperature.

Using format to boost comprehension

After you have made sure that:

■ You know who the main readers will be

■ Your document is logically organized

■ The content is complete

■ The technical level and document length are reasonable

■ The sentences are straightforward and clear

■ The jargon is explained...

...then you can think about using format devices to help readers find, scan, and digest information quickly. Remember: "format" does not mean "organization"; rather, it describes the document's "look" or "design".

Here are some format basics you can exploit effectively—even easily, with current software capabilities.

Keep your paragraphs short

Like long sentences, long paragraphs can tax and tire the reader.

Leave some "white space"

Don't pack the page. Overly dense pages of black type are uninviting to read.

Use descriptive headings

Headings that enhance your organizational framework and highlight your main points can help readers quickly grasp and follow the content. In fact, headings used liberally can form a "running summary" of your document. Thus, they can help readers scan, or focus on the sections of the text that interest them most.

Further, headings can be "weighted"—given more or less prominence—according to their relative importance in your outline. Conventionally, writers (or editors)_ mark headings as #1, 2, 3, etc., and assign specific type sizes, lettering styles (e.g., **bold face,** *italics*) or position (centered, flush left, "run-in") to each heading weight. Thus, the reader's grasp is doubly reinforced: first from scanning the headings, second from seeing how they relate in importance.

Use bullets to list key points

Often, you can't avoid long strings of conditions, caveats, results, or explanations. Instead of piling them into one huge, exhausting sentence, you can use "bullets"—dots at the beginning of a line—to signal terse, major points. Bullets are easy to grasp visually, especially if each point is no longer than a line. If necessary, you can emphasize key words (by underlining or **boldfacing**, for example), and continue with a brief explanation. That's exactly what we're doing on page 74 in the section *Devise "assists" for diverse readers.*

Use tables and graphics instead of statistics-laden text

Readers often have a hard time remembering or comparing many numbers written into a paragraph. Especially since experimental results often deal with huge amounts of numerical data, tables provide a far better means of presentation.

Some style and format tools you can tap to help readers grasp you message are:

- *use short paragraphs*

- *leave "white space" in the page layout*

- *write descriptive headings, "weighted" to reflect the document outline*

- *list key points using bullets*

- *put statistics in tables and figures*

They help readers compare and absorb the significance of the data quickly. Sometimes a simple graph, bar chart, pie chart, or other graphic display can summarize data even more strikingly.

Use tables to summarize complex content or comparisons

• place comparisons and summaries in tables

Tables, however, should not be limited to numbers: they are also an excellent form for summarizing comparative evaluations. For example, suppose your company is weighing the relative advantages of investing in several R&D options for future products. You are asked for your opinion. You could explore each option and write up the salient points. But the reader might still have difficulty comparing one option against another. You can facilitate this comparison by making a table:

1 Option	2 Main features	3 Advantages	4 Disadvantages	5 Risks	6 Rewards	7 Comments

Columns 2, 3, and 4 could list the technical evaluations, while columns 5 and 6 could deal with the business elements. Column 7, "comments", could cover any key points not dealt with in the other columns; it gives you room to break out of the tabular format—even to express your "gut" feeling for the option.

Here's an example of a table for summarizing comparisons.

Comparison of strengthening techniques

Strengthening method	Maximum attainable strengths (psi)	Advantages	Disadvantages	Actual applications
Elimination and minimization of surface defects	~ 500,000	• Simplicity and possible high speed • Low cost	• Requires subsequent protection from mechanical damage	• Glass fiber waveguides • Carbonated beverage bottles
Thermal tempering	~ 30,000	• Short process time • Applicable to most glasses • Relatively thick compressive zone • Low cost	• Thick glass required for optimum strengthening • Requires precise process control to avoid glass distortion • Shape limited	• Lenses • Auto windows • Architectural glass
High temperature chemical strengthening	~ 100,000	• Retains strength at higher use temperatures • Applicable to both thick and thin sections • Applicable to complex shapes	• Requires special glass composition • Relatively long process time as compared to thermal tempering • Possible thermal distortion of the ware • Disposal and handling	• Laboratory ware • Consumer ware • Spacecraft windows

Use diagrams with "cutlines" to replace or bolster descriptive text

Descriptions of technical concepts, devices, or processes are often awkward and difficult to follow. Simplify them for readers (and save yourself writing time) by using a clearly labeled diagram with a "cutline"—an explanatory caption based on the flow and terms used in the diagram. Here's an example.[8]

• describe processes and concepts through diagrams with detailed "cutlines"

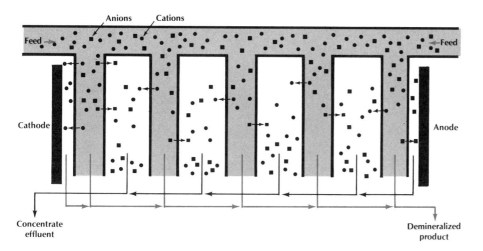

This schematic shows an electrodialysis system. When dc voltage is applied across the membrane pairs as the sample solution passes down through each of these pairs, cations pass through the cationic membrane on one side and anions through the anionic membrane on the other. As a result, ionic product is trapped in the compartments between membranes. These compartments are emptied together, their contents comprising the concentrate effluent. The other compartments are also emptied together, this stream comprising the demineralized product.

Place key illustrations and tables near the related text, NOT AT THE BACK of the document

In the age of the typist and illustrator, researchers often put all the text at the front of a document, and all the tables and diagrams at the back (all carefully numbered, of course!). But this system is cumbersome: if readers want to follow the illustrations, they have to constantly flip back and forth.

• integrate figures and tables with the text...

With today's computer software, we can integrate text, tables, and graphics. Thus, we can—and should—place "visuals" (tables, graphs, diagrams, or photos) as close as possible to the text they illustrate. This procedure greatly expedites the reader's grasp.

Accurately designate all tables, diagrams, and references

Aside from putting "visuals" as close as possible to the relevant text, you must designate them correctly. You can use a numbering system (Table 1, 2, etc.; Figure 1, 2, etc.); or you can say "the following table", "the figure above", "the diagram on page 23", whichever you prefer. If you need to use references, make sure they're numbered correctly and listed at the end of the chapter or at the end of the document. If you don't need to list the references, but want to cite a few sources, use footnotes.

and carefully designate them

But, put very specific details in appendices at the back

• use appendices for fine detail

...for example, printouts of lab results, equipment specifications, detailed series of spectra from chemical analyses, and other specialized data. However, be sure to help readers by telling them in the text on what page in the appendix they can find these detailed data. Then, on the "data" page, mention what page in the text the data refer to. Such simple techniques save the reader a lot of time. (We've followed our own advice by putting the detailed survey results at the back of the book, starting on page 139.)

Use CONSISTENT terminology in illustrations and text

• match terminology between illustrations and text

Besides using the same terms throughout your text, watch for consistency between terms in the text and the illustrations. Readers waste time (and become annoyed) when they plow through a tough technical explanation, refer to an "explanatory" diagram, and find that the terms in the diagram don't match those in the text!

Devise "assists" for diverse readers

• find ways to address readers at different levels:

Writing simultaneously for a broad range of readers—from specialist in the field, to skilled scientists, to manufacturing engineers, to marketers, to executives—is one of the most difficult problems that researchers face. If it's hard to figure out "what your manager really wants to know", as our survey shows, imagine how hard it is to write for a range of readers. Here are a few suggestions that help alleviate this problem by making needed information accessible to diverse readers.

- ■ As mentioned above, **develop a usable, fairly detailed table of contents** that is a **guide** to the reader.
- ■ **Use headings** liberally. (See page 71.)
- ■ **Use "headers" or "footers"** (chapter names at the top or bottom of the page) to tell the readers where they stand in the general scheme of your document.
- ■ **Put a top-notch summary** at the beginning of the document. This summary is useful for all readers. But for those farthest removed from your field, it may be the only part of the document they read. Because it may be the most widely read section, put time into writing it clearly and precisely.
- ■ **Write a brief, one paragraph abstract or capsule at the beginning of each chapter or section**. This capsule should supplement, but **not** repeat, the information in the "executive summary". A reader could then quickly scan each section, in addition to the executive summary, to obtain a little more information.
- ■ **Write "callouts" in the margin**—brief synopses that form a running summary of the text. They help the reader review the document quickly, yet obtain a clear picture of the contents. To use this technique (illustrated in much of this

book), you assign only a portion of the page to the text, and leave a wide margin for the callouts. Then, write the callouts beside the paragraphs they summarize. You can also use arrows in the margin to point out key lists of bulleted items in the text. You can even put diagrams in the margin. Then, readers have the option of:

- Reading the callouts straight through to get a good, quick summary of information

- Jumping over to the text whenever a point particularly interests them

- Jumping out of the text when it is too technical or lengthy

- Perusing the diagrams and tables in their proper context.

Further, a set of callouts is a litmus test of the organization and flow of a document: the callouts should read almost like an independent, succinct review of your document's main points.

Callouts in the margin should only be written **after** the document is finalized. However, this technique takes time to practice and polish. If you want to try it, fine; but we recommend giving this task to a professional writer or editor.

Give your document a facelift

Offer readers an easy-to-read typeface and layout, clear printing, and adequate binding. But, as one reviewer of this book remarked,

> "...remember that a glossy 'look' is not a substitute for concrete information. ...don't count on flashy design to rescue a document that's lacking in substance!"

Still, today's word-processing software packages and printers enable us to produce typeset-looking documents by offering wide choices in typeface, font, type size, margins, justification, columns, headings, and other features. However, beware of "over-formatting" that takes extra time to produce but does not help the reader. Graphic design professionals can help researchers—or departments—establish easy-to-follow formats, especially helpful for frequently produced documents.

Using designer advice, establish attractive, adaptable formats that enhance your message.

Always make sure the copies are legible and the pages in order. Finally, use a binding that can withstand the handling it will get. Don't staple a 200-page report, proposal, or manual!

All these design features will help readers grasp the material you write more easily. Use as many of them as you can.

DO LIST FOR RESEARCHERS

◼ Find out **who** your readers are and **how** they use your document

◼ Learn the double-5 organizational scheme

◼ Use double-5 to improve the quality of your writing by helping you:

- Get started on your writing task

- Outline your document

- Select needed information

- Decide on the right level of technical detail

- Write clearer, more focused documents

- Shorten your documents, yet

- Make your documents complete and logical

◼ Start writing more productively

- Use your computer advantageously for writing, revising, and editing

- Get used to writing via computer; beg or borrow one, or cajole your manager into buying you one

- Learn to plan your writing tasks realistically; iterate with your manager until you've agreed on **content** and **time** plans

- Revise your first draft for content only

- **Delegate** as much of your writing task as possible to editors, proofreaders, and others

- Master time management tips to protect your writing time

◼ Upgrade your language—start by correcting the nine most common pitfalls

◼ Use jargon sparingly; if you must use it, add definitions

◼ Help your readers grasp your intent ... use the format features that boost comprehension

◼ Take advantage of good writing instruction

◼ **Stop doing those writing tasks that don't require** your personal attention

◼ Read Chapter III to find out how managers can help you.

CHAPTER III

STEPS MANAGERS CAN TAKE

STEPS MANAGERS CAN TAKE

- **Immediate steps**—that only require reshuffling time and goals
- **Long-term steps**—that may need substantial planning and funding

Now that we have seen some steps researchers can take to improve their writing, let's look at actions managers can initiate to help researchers.

Some managers may be surprised to learn that they too must take action to improve researchers' writing. Or they may think their contribution is limited to finding teachers for writing courses.

Not so. Improving researchers' writing is not a one-way street. Without actively participating in solving researchers' writing difficulties, managers will continue having a hard time understanding what researchers write. Further, improvement in writing productivity and document quality will be limited from the outset.

Researchers will not go far on the path to writing improvement alone—they need managers' help to make major strides.

Let's look at both immediate and longer-term actions managers can take.

Immediate steps to take

Here are some suggestions you can start implementing right away.

As a manager, you can provide immediate help by:

Learn the double-5 organizational framework

If you haven't already read the section on document organization (pages 17 to 28), do it now. It provides a key tool for specifying what types of information you need in a document, and for analyzing and evaluating written products you receive. It also gives you a framework for pointing out where a document meets—or doesn't meet—those needs, and where additions or revisions are necessary. Most important: it provides common ground for communicating with researchers about writing tasks.

• understanding the double-5 approach to document organization...and employing this approach as you work with researchers

Provide precise guidelines
BEFORE writing begins

During the planning or "prewriting" stage, besides telling researchers **when** the document is due, you should spell out:

- ■ **Who** will need to see or use the document. This information can help researchers angle their material to make it more relevant and readable.

- ■ What types of information should be **emphasized.**

- ■ **How long** the document should be.

- ■ **How many pages** should be devoted to each part of the document. This simple guideline alone saves a lot of deliberation time: it helps researchers decide more quickly (and accurately) **how much technical detail** they can include.

• guiding researchers by spelling out:

You should also:

◼ Provide a short **outline** of the document, based on our organizational scheme, stressing the type of information needed.

◼ Give researchers **examples of quality documents** that can serve as models and guides.

Here is an example of guidelines researchers received in 1986 when they wrote articles for *Technology Sensor*—a newspaper-style publication B-TIP produced.

Battelle
Columbus Laboratories
505 King Avenue
Columbus, Ohio 43201
Telephone (614) 424-6424
Telex 24-5454

To Technology Sensor authors:

Thank you for agreeing to write an article for Technology Sensor. Your article will be read by a large group of corporate decision makers.

To help you prepare your article, focus on the technology and its business implications. Here's a generic outline you can adapt to your topic. The percentages indicate the weight you should give to each section.

15%   I.   **Problem and need.** What is the technical or market problem that the technology resolves, or the need it fulfills? What technological solutions have been attempted? Give us some background; set the stage.

       II.   **Solutions.** What is the best or most likely solution(s)? (Your technology subject, of course!) How does it work? What are the advantages, disadvantages, current status of development, future R&D needs? Perhaps you will include some case studies here as examples.

70-75%

       III. **Business implications.** What is the current status of commercialization for the technology? Who's using it? Why? Discuss potential business advantages and disadvantages of implementing the technology in terms of economics, companies most likely to benefit, and market impact.

10-15% IV.   **Outlook and opportunities.** What are the technological, economic, market and use trends in the near and long-term future? Can you supply a scenario of technological developments and industrial uses? What business opportunities and benefits will emerge--for suppliers and for users?

As you work on your article, remember:

* We would like to review the outline with you before you begin writing. We've found that this procedure ultimately saves everyone a great deal of time.
* Aim for 5 to 7 pages of double-spaced copy.
* Don't worry about style. To begin with, get all pertinent information on paper. You can even send us a transcript of your dictation.
* We'll polish the article, ask you a few questions, pass the draft back and forth to you a couple of times, and refine it until everyone is satisfied.
* Plan 1 to 3 visuals (photographs, diagrams, tables). Your diagrams can be rough sketches. Our designer will work with you to finalize visuals.
* You will have the opportunity to check the text and visuals before printing.

A recent edition of Technology Sensor is enclosed--to show you what we have in mind. We'll be calling you to set up an amenable schedule for your article.

Such guidance—even supervision—is crucial for newly hired staff and for researchers with weak writing skills. However, in smaller doses, it is equally important for researchers who are good writers.

Give clear, consistent guidelines

Be sure the directives you give researchers are clearly written and correctly understood. As one manager cautioned us, "Have you ever seen the memos managers write to researchers?" (Managers too can review the suggestions in Chapter II on *Steps researchers can take* to improve the clarity of their writing.) Try also to maintain consistency: changing your mind about what is needed in a document wastes time and only contributes to a major problem for researchers—figuring out what the manager really wants to know.

Review the outlines of documents...

...especially of longer tasks, to make sure the information and emphases meet your and other readers' needs. Use the double-5 scheme to check for completeness of content. Iterate with the researchers until you've hammered out a satisfactory, workable outline. Then, help them devise a plan to manage their writing time effectively.

• carefully reviewing outlines and helping researchers improve them

Give researchers useful feedback on CONTENT...

...particularly after the first draft. Tell them, for example, where information is too detailed, lacking, unclear, or difficult to understand.

• providing constructive comments on content...

But, to be useful, your comments should be constructive and specific. For example, you could:

- Point out **exactly** where technical descriptions are vague or unclear
- Ask **precise** clarification questions (e.g., "On page 2, line 17: What is the meaning of this statement?")
- Make **constructive** suggestions for improving content (e.g., "On page 5, you could give an example about ABC".)
- Describe how readable the document was—and specify where the going was particularly tough.

Such feedback is important. In fact, one researcher claimed "... it is the most important factor in helping me produce good documents".

But avoid becoming an editor—especially of language. Such editing should not be the manager's job—although our survey shows some 57 percent of managers sometimes do it. Further, researchers often resent a manager's editing. As one researcher commented,

without editing language—it's not your job

> "... I have no problem with (my manager's) suggestions. But unilateral corrections or changes drive me up the wall, especially if a document goes out under my signature."

Another pointed out:

> "There is a considerable amount of editing by my manager—but it is not necessarily due to a problem with content or organization,

but because he likes his writing style better than mine. Interestingly, though, his style is haughty, pompous sounding, and fraught with grammatical errors."

Some managers are already sensitive to this situation. For example, one manager wrote:

"The writer knows what the general topic is. If the product is anywhere close to what is needed, I don't change it as I believe in protecting their pride of authorship. If it is not close, then I will suggest changes. I don't make changes because an ''if I know so much about it—why don't I write it in the first place' syndrome would result. I want it to be a 'his/her' effort rather than an 'our' effort."

• giving encouraging feedback regularly

Feedback should also be consistently forthcoming—and encouraging. True, managers usually give "problems" top priority; the "good stuff" doesn't require immediate attention. However, this attitude, taken to the extreme, can be demoralizing. Look at what one researcher wrote:

"If he dislikes the product, then he hits me (verbally, not physically). If he likes it, he ignores me (he says he is concentrating on 'The Real Problems')."

On the other hand, don't just give pats-on-the-back. One researcher mused:

"I'm usually told when a piece of writing was 'good'—there's usually no other feedback; so I don't know if 'no news' is really 'bad news' or just acceptable and unmemorable."

But managers got good marks from several researchers who noted: "My manager makes positive comments".

Help researchers plan their writing time

Here's an area where your immediate help is a must. Some researchers are skilled at organizing their time. But many need assistance and even moral support—both in planning their writing time and in protecting the time they have scheduled. As managers, you can help by:

• helping researchers plan and protect their writing time by:

- Ensuring that planning for a document starts early.

- Reviewing the outline **before** the writing effort begins, to make certain the content is right.

- Reviewing the researchers' time plan for writing the document to make sure it is reasonable. Be especially wary of underestimating the time needed to do quality work. (For more details, you can review our guidelines to researchers on realistic time estimation procedures. See page 47.)

- Keeping a copy of researchers' writing schedules. When they're in a writing mode, touch base with them frequently—but only during their non-writing hours. Make sure everyone respects the schedule and **no one** (not even you!) interrupts.

During the work, if problems crop up that demand changes in schedules or even in outlines, **deal with them immediately;** don't wait till the document is completed.

Planning for "quiet" space is another problem managers must help resolve. Several managers noted this difficulty. One wrote: "Our open offices are a major deterrent to concentration on report preparation." Another said, "...very poor surrounding for report writing: too noisy, hard to concentrate."

• providing "quiet space".

However, this problem can be alleviated: for example, some companies provide quiet conference rooms or "writing lounges"; others have cubicles in the library.

Many researchers commented that they write at home just to have uninterrupted time. As an alternative, managers might encourage the use of "flextime" to ensure quiet. However, the best solution is for researchers to have private offices where a closed door helps keep out unwanted noise and uninvited "visitors".

Steps to implement over the longer term

All suggestions we've made so far are actions managers can implement right away. True, substantial improvements in quality, readability, and time can emerge. But quantum productivity gains and vastly superior documents can only result from a far reaching review of the writing process and introduction of creative, longer term actions.

You also need to take long-term actions.

Here are some fundamental steps managers should investigate, weigh—and start implementing.

Streamline writing requirements

One manager commented to the author on the aim of our survey:

> "I am satisfied with the steps we take now to help writing quality. You are focusing on the writer and his skills. (But) I would ask: Is the problem in what we ask them to write" **Do we ask for too much too often?** For too much in-depth analysis when all we need is a description of work done? **My people complain that they have too much to write.** If that is true, how can any of it be high quality?"

To overcome excessive writing demands—as one manager described—

Writing requirements can be streamlined in four ways:

evaluate ways of streamlining writing requirements:

■ Reduce the amount of information researchers need to communicate in each document

■ Reduce the number of documents researchers need to write

■ Cut back the number of reviews—and subsequent revisions—a document undergoes

■ Simplify researchers' writing tasks.

To do so, you will need to examine closely:

■ **What information** you need—and what you don't need.

■ **How frequently** you need this information. Particularly, take a hard, hard look at researchers' "regular" reporting requirements. Identify and eliminate rigid "busywork" reporting—e.g., on some tasks, weekly "progress reports" cannot reflect enough progress to be worth the time they take to write...and read.

■ What **purpose and use** each required document will serve.

"Generic outlines" will help, particularly with periodic reports.

Then, as much as possible, develop easy-to-use **"generic outlines" or "macros"**. These outlines should meet your needs, or other users' or clients' needs, while simplifying researchers writing tasks.

This outlining step applies especially to progress and final project reports, and to frequently used types of documents, e.g., proposals, memos, business letters, or evaluations of potential projects or products. Outlines could also be geared to specific audiences—e.g., senior management, R&D planners, program managers, or peers. These generic outlines could even be a precise series of questions, with estimated space for answers. Answering a series of questions (which can be developed according to our organizational scheme's prompts) is far faster than originating an entire document.

Monthly progress reports may only require answers to a subset of double-5 questions:

These outlines don't always need to contain all parts of our double-5 scheme. A case in point: a program manager we interviewed already knows the goals, scope, and planned overall solution of the work. Further, conclusions are written up in quarterly reports to the client. Thus for monthly progress reports, this manager asks researchers to answer four questions:

1. What did you accomplish last month (results)?
2. Were there any major problems (both technical and operational)?
3. What do you expect to accomplish next month (immediate "solution" tasks)?
4. Do you anticipate any major problems?

The responses typically take 10 to 20 lines on one page. (If the response to items 1 and 3 is "As planned", and to items 2 and 4, "None", the monthly report would take only 4 lines!)

For **external documents**, do a similar evaluation and try to negotiate streamlined written "deliverables". However, the client may specify the outline of a proposal or final report. For all major documents, try to eliminate redundancies in the review process—a key time grabber.

Though streamlining may require significant coordination and effort to implement...

Implementing this approach division-wide requires coordination among several managers and managerial levels. It also requires sitting down with researchers and editors to decide on generic outlines or models of frequently needed document types. It means holding discussions with all research groups so that the purpose of these models is clear: simplifying writing tasks—not adding document-uniformity burdens. It means leaving the door open to further discussion—viewing this approach as a continuing refinement process. It may even mean setting up a "written communications committee", including both researchers and managers, that will promote writing productivity via streamlining. The committee's objective would be: "Find ways for researchers to write less—but better...so managers can learn more—in less time".

the results will simplify writing tasks and improve communication.

Make computers available and encourage their use

Providing computers and encouraging their use...

Researchers won't require much encouragement: as our survey shows, many of them are eager to write via computer. Without exception, all the researchers who use a computer tell us it has increased their productivity enormously.

Furthermore, even scientists who do know how to keyboard (formerly called touch typing!) may enjoy writing via computer. One says,

> "When I compose, I'm thinking slowly and trying to be accurate. So it's no problem to keep up with my hunt and peck typing method."

Another researcher reports:

> "It's wonderful—I'm so prolific. You should see how fast I can go with three fingers!"

Computers can have a triple positive impact on

■ Help improve writing quality

■ Reduce researchers' time to write a higher quality document

■ Reduce secretaries' time for completing document production

Drafts do not have to be entered into a word processor by an operator, since the work can be printed out automatically when the researcher is finished writing. Check the researchers' section on using computers (page 43) for more details on how these improvements are attained.

Computers can be made available to researchers in several ways. Ideally, researchers should have their own workstations or network hookups. This option is becoming commonplace as hardware prices decline. In the meanwhile, several alternatives are possible. In rising order of preference they are:

Ideally, each researcher should have a computer,

but as alternatives you can:

◄

■ Allocate a room or two with computers and printers dedicated to a small group of researchers. With this option, however, accessibility is limited: the computer is usually in such high demand that researchers have to wait their turn. Furthermore, they have to drag all their notes and other materials to the computer room.

■ Designate a large space as a "writing room", with library-style quiet rules. Set apart sections (with freestanding, sound absorbing walls) for several computers.

■ Buy several laptops or notebook computers that researchers can use in their offices, at home, or in a vacant room during their writing periods.

But be on the alert for new technological aids. Available and emerging hardware and software could substantially reduce costs for communications, data access, planning, writing improvement, graphics, proofreading, and publishing. (For more details, turn to page 126 in Chapter VI, "*Outlook*".)

Hire a technical editor

Though researchers can improve gradually as "self-editors", a technical editor can speed progress dramatically for two of our three writing goals:

■ **Upgrading the quality** of the written product

■ **Reducing the amount of time** researchers spend on producing documents.

Technical editors can upgrade document quality, reduce researchers' time on documents,

From the cost-benefit view, professional editors offer a quick return on investment. First, because the cost per hour for technical editors is less than for researchers, immediate savings accrue: researchers spend less time on writing tasks; an editor does these tasks more quickly. Second, as mutual understanding grows between researchers and an editor, savings are likely to increase. Third, if the editor is encouraged to help individual researchers pinpoint their writing problems and "discover" remedies, researchers can learn to upgrade the quality of their original drafts. This improvement, in turn, shortens the researcher's, editor's, and manager's review tasks.

...and provide cost benefits.

However, to achieve these benefits—

■ The right editor must be chosen for the specific group

■ Researchers must have positive attitudes about editorial help

■ The tasks and goals of the editor and the researchers must be clearly delineated

■ Workable, effective operating guidelines must be established.

To achieve these goals, you must:

Let's look briefly at each of these elements—and then see how one department at Battelle implemented this step.

Choose the right editor

Because of the type and amount of contact an editor will have with researchers, finding the right person is the key to success. As one researcher commented: "I have encountered some editors who are only marginally effective and it can take longer to explain the task than simply doing the work myself."

• choose the right editor—

To select competent editors, first make sure the candidates have the **right editorial skills** for your group. Ask them how they would handle your group's specific writing problems. Let them show you how they have dealt with similar difficulties in the past. Look at samples of their previous work—both corrected copy and the final product.

one with the right skills and background,

If possible, choose a candidate with a **science background**—or at least with editorial experience in your group's area. Such background immediately puts the editor a step ahead in gaining researchers' confidence and in understanding the scientific goals they are trying to pursue. A background in business communications is also a plus.

Finally, select a candidate who has **good "interpersonal" skills**—a person who generates cooperation, goodwill, and credibility. Editors must have empathy for the researcher's creative role in the research process. They must also understand the researcher's difficulties in communicating new scientific information to non-specialist managers whose background may be in a totally different field. Editors need to be flexible—and know how to deal sensitively with each individual. But they also need to clearly understand managers' requirements.

who can adapt to each researcher's needs...

...and the manager's requirements

Help researchers develop positive attitudes

Although many researchers appreciate the assistance editors can give them, many are leery about any outside help. The reasons? Some cannot overcome the "close to the vest" syndrome: they believe a person must be associated directly with the work to communicate it. They may not trust the judgment of the editor. Others feel they will be nit-picked about minute, unimportant details. In some organizations, researchers may be concerned about maximizing the percent of time they spend on project work.

Likewise, some managers doubt the value of editors. One manager claimed that using editors is a "bandaid approach": ..."researchers never will learn to write properly because someone is always there to 'fix it' for them". In fact, the reverse is true. Researchers will never learn to write better if no one is telling them—in a positive way—where they are falling short. With an editor "fixing" their writing, and showing them why changes are made, researchers have an excellent one-on-one opportunity to learn **exactly** what's wrong with their writing and how they can 'fix it' themselves.

• realize that with proper guidance and information, an editor can produce accurate technical/business writing

Changing such attitudes is a long-term process. The most persuasive catalyst for change: successful results.

Spell out the editor's tasks and goals...

...it will help alleviate researchers' anxieties and reservations; it will prevent disappointments; it will encourage "let's give it a try" attitudes. For example, editors' goals and tasks could be broadly defined as:

• clearly define editorial tasks and goals—e.g., they might be:

- Helping researchers produce clear, relevant documents. The editor's task is not to completely rewrite a document, and, in the process, mutilate the researcher's pride of authorship.

- Assuring document quality, completeness, and readability. As non-specialists, editors can also assess how well other non-specialists will understand the technical explanations.

- Maintaining technical accuracy, yet assuring clear language.

- Showing the researcher precisely what changes and clarifications they suggest. This process offers a natural opportunity for researchers to improve their writing skills and for editors to hone their technology awareness.

■ Individually coaching researchers who have tough writing problems.

Exactly what the editor will or will not do must be specified. For example:

■ Will the editor be responsible for obtaining or even preparing graphics or other visuals?

■ Will the editor be responsible for obtaining all the needed approvals before a document is completed or sent to a client?

■ Or will such tasks be negotiable for individual projects?

In the upcoming example, starting on page 90, you'll see a detailed job description.

Establish workable, effective, operating guidelines

• establish workable guidelines on

Decisions are needed on several issues:

Will the editor's services be used on a compulsory or a voluntary basis? The guideline might be: researchers are free to decide whether, when, and at what stage they want to use the editor's services. Alternatively, project managers might decide that all researchers on that project should work with the editor. Another possible guideline: all documents distributed outside the company must first go through the editor. Or, line managers might decide which documents need editing—perhaps according to the document's importance or the previous writing performance of the researchers.

who will use the editor,

Who will pay for the editor's service? Many arrangements are possible. In our example (see page 90), the editor essentially runs an entrepreneurial business; she must "pay her way" from the hourly fees she "charges" researchers. This option has the advantage of bringing the costs and benefits immediately to light: the editor can estimate how much time a certain job is likely to take; the researchers can calculate whether that cost is a worthwhile tradeoff for their savings in time and for probable improvements in quality.

who will pay for the editor, and

However, this approach has a serious flaw: often, the researcher who is the poorest writer is the last to voluntarily ask for editorial help. Thus, it cannot guarantee overall quality improvement for a group's writing efforts. This drawback is particularly obvious when several researchers contribute to one document.

Another option: the line-group could cover the editor's salary, assign certain types of jobs on a regular basis, allow flexibility for fitting in "voluntary" work, and have the editor instruct those with serious writing problems if time is available.

A third option is to "write the editor into" project costs. As a member of the project team, the editor can also help decide on efficient procedures for "engineering" the report—e.g., developing schedules, assigning writing tasks, qualifying and quantifying each contributor's inputs, and defining the editor's role. Increasingly, proposal requests—both from industry and government—require inclusion of editorial costs. One manager noted, "...this approach is the best—the one I usually use".

where the editor will enter the writing process.

At what point in the document's evolution will the editor's services be used? Here again, several routes are open. But remember: the earlier in the document development process that the editor is included, the better the final document is apt to be. Thus, if you call in an editor at the last minute "to save" a disastrous report, the most that person can do is to scan quickly for typos, punctuation, inconsistencies in figure and table numbers, or other similar, **non-content**, functions.

On the other hand, if editors participate from the early outline stage, they can help shape the content, organization, level of detail, orientation, length, and emphasis at the outset—the **crucial content** elements.

However, review these guidelines. As understanding and confidence grow between researchers and the editor, operating guidelines can be revised to maximize benefits from the editor's services.

Delegate document review tasks to the editor

Thoroughly discuss your criteria for various documents with the editor—types of information, emphasis, slant, length, and level of technical and business detail. With these criteria, the editor can gradually relieve you of many editorial review difficulties quickly...and can also suggest practical solutions.

An editor can also relieve you of many review tasks.

Now, go to the next page to see an example.

MANAGER'S OFFICE

MANAGER'S OFFICE

EDITOR'S OFFICE

WHY and HOW a department integrated a technical editor

In 1986, one of Battelle's departments had employed a technical editor for almost 5 years. To get a closer look at how this position operated, we interviewed:

- The department manager
- A program manager
- A researcher
- The editor.

Here's the picture we got.

The department manager

This department manager decided to employ an editor for two main reasons:

1. Quality of both proposals and reports was less than he wanted.

2. Too many "high-priced" researchers were proofreading, writing executive summaries, and doing similar non-research tasks.

The department looked for an applicant with:

- English competence and editing experience
- Interpersonal skills: ability to communicate and work with researchers
- Ability to look at **what** is said, not just **how** it is said
- Ability to "homogenize a document": put out a well-integrated product, even though the document was "written by committee".

They looked for a candidate with "some acquaintance" with the physical sciences; but they did even better. They found an editor with a BA in Physics, who was working on a Ph.D. in English.

They used a "no imposition" system. It meant the editor had to sell her services; she had to prove her value to the researchers by saving them time and producing superior documents that didn't get sent back for redos. However, even though the editor was assigned full time to this department, she actually reported to a central Editorial Group

which was part of Battelle's Proposal and Report Production Department. She kept track of her own hours. If her time was not fully spent on projects, the downtime was covered by the central Editorial Group.

The editor fulfilled several tasks. She needed to:

- Write executive summaries for reports
- Critically review documents and management presentations
- Offer suggestions on content and organization of documents
- Regularly edit and produce major reports for some large, key projects; she was "written into" these projects
- Act as a liaison between the department and the central Report Production group for word processing, typesetting, and printing services
- Write a biannual newsletter, mass-mailed to clients
- Write articles for Battelle's internal weekly newsletter
- Write biosketches and similar items, and keep them on disk
- Review high-visibility management memos and reports.

The result from the manager's view: "A dramatic rise in quality". The documents became better organized and more readable. The sentences were not endlessly long. Style, consistency, spelling, and format were properly handled. By relieving managers and researchers of much work and reliably producing superior documents, she built a constituency; many researchers "swore by her". Feedback was so favorable that, if she became overloaded with work, the department manager claimed he would hire another editor. (In fact, he later did so.)

The program manager

This program manager needed to provide high quality, quarterly reports on a large, multi-year project. To achieve these goals, he decided it would be mandatory to use an editor. The system worked as follows:

- The six principal investigators gave the program manager their raw material, including text and figures
- The program manager reviewed this material briefly and gave it to the editor
- She edited the report and interfaced with all the technical people to make sure all parts were there and to resolve any questions
- She created the abstract and the executive summary, subject to the program manager's approval

In this manager's view, editorial services are so important to quality assurance that their use should be compulsory. Then, the problem of "convincing researchers" would be avoided. He believed strongly that the editor's job should be viewed as an integral part of a project, and that time and costs should be budgeted accordingly.

■ She then put the report into final form: inserted figures and tables, proofread, and obtained approvals

■ The program manager then reviewed the final version of the report prior to printing and binding.

The program manager thought that the editor's scientific background was helpful in providing complete, technically accurate reports. The results were excellent. The quality of the reports rose: readability improved, and errors decreased. The number of researcher-hours needed for the review process was drastically reduced. Since the cost for the editor's time was half or a third of the scientists' charge-out rate, the savings were appreciable. Simultaneously, the scientists could devote more time to research. Thus, their productivity increased.

Another major source of savings on these reports was the widespread use of the computer. Almost all the inputs to the editor were computer written. This procedure gave the editor better copy, eliminated the need for a secretary to transcribe handwritten copy that was often hard to read, and put an end to major retyping. This program manager recommended making computers available to all technical people.

Taken together, the editor and computer input provided outstanding cost reductions: **the cost for a report was cut in half**.

The program manager also noted that improvements in researchers' writing skills were marginal—largely because "instructing researchers" was not defined as one of the editor's tasks. However, he thought that the department should support such instruction, particularly for the editor's "repeat" customers.

A major reason this program manager was convinced of the editor's value: the unquestionably improved quality of the document paid for itself in the better impression on the client, and in the higher potential acceptance of future research proposals.

The researcher

This active researcher had a high workload. He began using the editor's services because:

■ He needed someone to "take the ball and run" after he completed a handwritten draft of a document's contents—i.e., an editor who could take original copy and deliver a final product

■ His report budgets were low

■ He needed to produce quality documents, since "the report is the product"

■ He had to find ways to write cost effectively.

Not only did he ask the editor to improve the writing and do all the other editorial tasks, he also made her aware of the time and cost constraints. He found her sensitive to these needs—and resourceful in finding ways to reduce costs.

He was extremely satisfied with the results. Though he considered himself a good writer, his participation after the first draft was minimal. All the hours the editor put into his documents were hours gained for his research. Further, relations with his clients improved because the reports were always on time and of high quality. But above all, the editor's services relieved him of the enormous worry and burden of completing large quantities of written work to meet frequent deadlines.

For example, during a particular 2-month period, several reports and proposals had to be completed. This researcher had to spend 80 percent of his time writing. In this mode, he never would have been able to meet all the deadlines without the editor. Over the entire year, he estimates, the editor saved from 20 to 30 percent of his time. He saw at least a 10 percent improvement in the final quality of the product.

The main limitation he faced in using the editor's service was the competition for her time! Other researchers in the department started to catch on, so she was almost always overloaded.

This researcher saw several advantages in having an editor attached to the department and located in the same area. First, it was more convenient. Second, the editor could learn the technologies and become even more useful as a "content evaluator".

In fact, this researcher believed there is hardly a sizable research group that would not benefit from a technical editor because:

- Many secretaries are already overworked; coordinating the production of reports is an added burden
- Researchers would have more time for science
- Researchers would be "treated as professional scientists" —a good morale booster.

But he believed researchers should be persuaded of the benefits, not forced to use an editor's services. Thus, if departments do decide to hire an editor, they should have several meetings to explain realistically how the editor can help and to encourage researchers to see for themselves.

He strongly suggested including instruction as one of the editor's tasks—especially for newly hired researchers. Also, because of editors' experience in many tasks with many kinds of clients, he thought editors could helpfully advise researchers on:

- How to orient documents
- How long documents should be
- Where to get relevant information or examples for producing a document tailored to a particular client. In fact, the editor could act as a clearing house for different readers and clients.

To decide whether hiring an editor is worthwhile, each group or department would have to estimate the expected demand for the editor, evaluate its staff's writing skills and time use, and arrive at a cost-benefit conclusion. To this researcher, the editor became indispensable; she became integral to his ability to maintain a high level of research productivity.

The editor

The editor in this department saw her goals as:

- **Facilitating** the production of researchers' documents
- **Serving** researchers according to their individual document's needs.

SOMEWHERE — HIDDEN IN ALL OF THESE WORDS — IS A POINT SOMEONE IS TRYING TO MAKE!

EDITOR

She interpreted "facilitating" both as improving the usefulness of the final reports and as getting documents completed more quickly and on time.

However, she faced many varied problems in trying to fulfill these functions. Sometimes, the manager or author was dissatisfied with a final report—and she was just told to "fix it". But often the people in the lab didn't have time to give her the inputs for "fixing it". Many documents she received were "ungrammatical, turgid, and boring". Further, she often had to plow through 15 pages until she came to the guts of the document. Then, the emphasis was apt to change from paragraph to paragraph—almost at whim. Sometimes, information was missing. The most common omissions were:

- Conclusions and implications from results
- Explanations of **why** researchers did something, not just **what** they did.

She noted that new people were particularly worried about entrusting their work to anyone else; they seemed to equate overzealously writing an overlong report with excellence in performing their jobs.

So what did she try to do when researchers came to her for editorial help? Depending on the specific problems or requests, she might:

- Review the document's organization to make sure it is in logical order.
- Look over all the sections of the document to make sure it is complete.
- Check the document—both text and illustrations—for consistency in content, terms, and style; contradictions; and bizarre words.
- Shorten the document whenever possible.
- Write an executive summary.

■ Improve the sentence structure and overall style so that the document is "at least reasonably readable".

■ Help interpret requests for proposals (RFPs). (By the way, she notes that they too are often poorly written and hard to understand...). In effect, she helps interpret what the client wants to hear.

■ Try to help researchers develop a "sense of audience". Says she, ..."This is one of my most important jobs. After all, you can teach a monkey to punctuate!".

■ Act as a "hotline" consultant: researchers she works with often phone her for answers to questions on specific usage, style, grammar, and semantics.

■ Pull a whole report together when sections are written by several researchers. Her tasks might range from editing, to pushing the document through all the production and proofreading steps. Her work for the program manager (described above) is an example. She receives input from six people and cranks out the final copy—complete with executive summary. The program manager only sees the original and final copy—unless some program emphasis question arises that needs to be resolved in the interim.

How did she go about her task? First, as a free agent, she needed to find work. So she "grubbed around" the lab to find out what needed to be written. She told researchers she would work on their documents in whatever form they were submitted. (She sometimes even worked from lab books!) However, she encouraged researchers to use a computer and give her the disks—because they were the easiest and fastest input form to handle.

She showed and explained her revisions to researchers. Indirectly, this process helped researchers improve their writing. She was always conscious of not changing the meaning; so she checked with researchers. She also made a list of specific points that needed clarification and suggested ways to improve the document as a whole. To speed up repetitive writing tasks, she standardized certain proposal formats and established a computerized "biosketch bank".

The results were encouraging. People seemed satisfied with the documents. The number of researchers who used her services constantly increased—in fact she had to delegate some of her "overflow" to other editors. More people asked her to get involved earlier in a document's development, some even at the outline stage.

More precisely, after almost 5 years as editor in this department of 80, she was working with about 60 percent of the researchers:

- closely with six
- regularly with 10 or more
- on an "as needed" basis with the rest.

In that year, for example, she worked on:

No. of documents	Type of document	Percent time
32	Reports, mostly multi-authored	48
13	Technical papers and articles	20
10	Various departmental needs: e.g., capability statements, newsletters, marketing items	15
7	Proposals	11
4	Extra work outside the department	6

Also, she assumed a major responsibility in a large project: she edited reports at the clients' various sites around the country. The clients responded enthusiastically to having an editor on site. In fact, they then wanted an editor assigned to all similar project contracts.

She was gratified that many people asked her questions about language. Though she did not expressly instruct researchers (except for one individual, at the request of his manager), she saw improved drafts from some people. She also noticed a growing sensitivity to the needs of the reader. But above all, she was most pleased that her clients—both researchers and managers—no longer worried whether their documents "made it" on schedule. She facilitated their work, saved them time, and reduced frustration.

With this experience, her recommendations for departments thinking about hiring a technical editor were:

■ Editors must have management support and backing

■ During the hiring process, editors must be given a clear idea of how they are expected to function, for example:

- What the main focus of their efforts will be

- Whether every document will go through the editorial mill, or just a selected subset

- Whether researchers will choose to use these editorial services (except when the manager explodes!)

- Whether editors have to dig up work for themselves

- What expectations managers have.

■ When they come on board, editors should speak to groups of researchers, explain what they can do to help, and discuss how they will go about their job. Researchers have to be convinced that an editor will save them time and money.

And what does it take to be an editor in a research group? She believes it requires an ability to help people; friendliness; and an empathy for scientists. It requires an analytical mind and familiarity with terminology. It requires knowing rules of style, usage, grammar, and punctuation to justify changes. Of course, it requires confidence. Yet, it also requires modesty, a willingness to learn...and a well developed sense of humor!

Establish writing courses geared to technical/business needs

Many companies, according to our survey, have given researchers the opportunity to attend writing courses—both in-house and at neighboring institutions. Some 35 percent of the researchers reported attending such courses. Yet the results have been disappointing overall: though most researchers and managers agreed that some improvement occurred, 40 percent of the managers described it as "minor". Furthermore, several managers commented that researchers often did not take advantage of available courses.

Why have these courses not enjoyed greater success? Perhaps because they:

- Were not geared to the researchers' main problems
- Were not oriented to the managers' needs in that company
- Did not provide follow-up.

Researchers can profit from writing courses that:

Yet, properly designed courses can be an effective way to upgrade and hone researchers' writing, if they:

- Focus on researchers' actual work...to make the instruction immediately useful and relevant
- Deal with the main writing problems researchers actually have. Many problems instructors conventionally cover may not be important for the technical/business documents researchers write and managers read.

Types of instruction

These needs can be met through group or individual instruction, or even "self-teaching". Each type has its ground rules, advantages, and limitations.

One approach uses group instruction. But:

For **group** instruction to succeed, some ground rules are:

- The groups must be small enough (say, 10–20) for the instructor to pay attention to each individual
- Instructors should base the course on our survey results: it should focus primarily on problems in **content;** second, on methods to improve writing **strategies and procedures;** third, on **language** "habits" that obstruct rapid comprehension.

However, the instructor must adapt the course structure to the specific issues in content, strategies, and language that are problematic for the researchers in each group. Thus, the instructor needs to uncover those particular problems.

and:

Additional criteria for success are:

- Instructors must find out precisely what the managers need to learn from researchers' documents and what these managers view as the chief barriers to understanding.
- Within the framework we've suggested, instructors must have the flexibility to tailor the course to the needs of both researchers and managers.
- The course should be sufficiently concentrated to maintain momentum; but it must also build-in adequate time for researchers to discuss their individual questions and to practice what they've learned.

Managers should also attend a similar course, angled to their perspective. When managers and researchers are on the same "wavelength", progress speeds up vastly.

Group courses offer some important advantages for researchers.* First, researchers discover they are not alone in their written communication difficulties. (This revelation immediately encourages participants and boosts morale.) Second, they can often pick up creative solutions from their colleagues. Third, they gain an understanding of other researchers' difficulties and start thinking about "broader" solutions.

Group instruction offers researchers helpful interaction.

However, group courses may be difficult to schedule. Also, each researcher will probably expend more time than in individual instruction.

Individual instruction, on the other hand, can be tailored exactly to each researcher's needs. Scheduling is also more flexible. But, while individual teaching may take less of the researcher's time, it will demand much more of the instructor's time for the same number of researchers.

Individual instruction can meet researchers' specific needs more flexibly,

but takes more of the instructor's time.

This method will likely be effective only if firm, monitored study programs and instruction timetables are established. Individual "lessons" should be scheduled closely so "measurable" progress can be made.

Occasionally this approach doesn't succeed because the individual researchers feel they are being singled out for a terrible deficiency—a feeling that would vaporize in a group!

Whether you decide on group or individual instruction, make sure that regular follow-up is part of the instruction package. For a period after the course, researchers should have access to the instructor to continue resolving their writing problems and improving their writing products. Also, researchers should have their workload lessened during the course; they must have time to digest and assimilate what they've learned.

In either case, regular follow-up is essential to real progress.

---

* Note that these same advantages also apply to managers!

Self-teaching, a low-cost approach,

can be effective in the right circumstances.

"Self-teaching", a low-cost study mode, can sometimes work, especially for the mechanical aspects of writing. For the more difficult areas of content and strategies, self-teaching can be effective for those researchers who are already aware of their writing difficulties and who are actively seeking to improve. In fact, one of our aims in writing this book is to offer practical ideas researchers can implement **on their own**. However, progress will likely be faster if this effort is integrated with an instructor.

An optimum approach would combine all three instruction modes.

An optimum solution might be to start with group courses, and continue with individual instruction—or even monitored "self teaching"—as the follow-up. Such a system would assure reinforcement of learned skills, and would utilize the advantages of all three teaching modes.

How should course groups be organized?

A simple way to offer writing courses is to notify researchers of course dates and application criteria via a memo or the company newsletter.

However, our survey indicates that certain groups of researchers may tend to have similar problems.[*] Thus, managers might consider setting up courses for specific categories of researchers. The groups should be sufficiently homogeneous for instructors to build effective courses and for researchers to reap maximum benefits. For example, courses might target groups of:

Writing courses might target specific groups, such as:

▶

- ■ New hires
- ■ Researchers from similar disciplines—e.g., chemists, mechanical engineers, electrical engineers, biologists, metallurgists
- ■ Staff in one research section
- ■ Relatively poor writers who need a lot of help...who must almost start from scratch

---

[*] This indication is based on a preliminary look at the impact on survey results of researchers' area of specialization or length of work experience.

■ Competent writers who want to improve their skills

■ Researchers who need to produce certain kinds of documents—e.g., progress reports on research; final reports; reports to upper management; proposals; memos and business letters; evaluations of proposed projects.

Companies might also decide to establish courses for managers who need to be more active in guiding researchers—e.g., in developing generic outlines, managing time, streamlining writing requirements, introducing computers and other technological aids, utilizing editorial assistance, and writing clear guideline memos to researchers. Our survey shows some support for this idea.

...and even managers who will be guiding researchers.

Some managers might themselves enjoy a course on how to write R&D digests or evaluations for top management or clients!

Who will instruct courses?

This question, obviously, has no pat answer—especially since many previous courses have not proven effective.

Instructors could be drawn from in-house editors, university teachers, or competent outside consultants. The important point is to recruit instructors with extensive **practical** experience, who are tuned in to managers' and researchers' precise needs. Companies may even need to train people for this task.

Course instructors, above all, should have extensive practical experience.

Clearly, effective courses can be an important tool to help researchers improve their technical/business writing skills. But they also demand a significant investment of thought and funds. Because such courses can attack the roots of writing weaknesses, they can have far-reaching, positive impacts on writing habits, capabilities, and products. Thus, they can yield valuable returns in writing skills, quality, productivity—and satisfaction—both for researchers and managers.

Use performance reviews to improve researchers' writing

Almost 60 percent of the managers responding to our survey favored "including improved writing skills as a positive factor in performance evaluations". In fact, managers indicated it was the tool they were most willing to use to upgrade researchers' writing. Since writing occupies about 30 percent of researchers' time, writing performance indeed is a valid area to review.[*]

For many researchers, writing is a legitimate item to evaluate;

But the most important reason to review writing performance is to offer researchers an **incentive** to improve their writing skills and products.

but its inclusion in performance reviews should offer incentives to improve writing skills.

The responses from our survey prompted some sticky questions about the structure and implications of such a review. For example:

However, several questions must be answered first:

■ How will writing areas needing improvement be selected?

■ What help will researchers get to implement these improvements?

■ How will these improvements be evaluated?

■ How much weight will the writing factor carry in the total performance rating and for future advancement?

[*] An MIT study of an R&D group points out that in that group's "Appraisal Review Form", only 1 out of 22 criteria for employee job performance dealt explicitly with "communications abilities". Yet, "communications abilities had much more weight than 1/22 of the total because supervisors rated employees for other categories by referring to employees' documents". See reference 1.

Here are some suggestions that may help you structure a more objective and useful review. Many are based on the insightful comments made by managers and researchers.

To provide an effective incentive, "writing improvement" cannot be some vague idea or subjective notion. As much as possible, the review should be constructive, quantitative, and achievable. As in other performance review areas, managers and researchers should come to an agreement by:

Managers and researchers should agree on writing performance criteria by:

1. Identifying the specific areas needing improvement

2. Setting goals for the researchers

3. Delineating actions to help the researcher achieve these goals

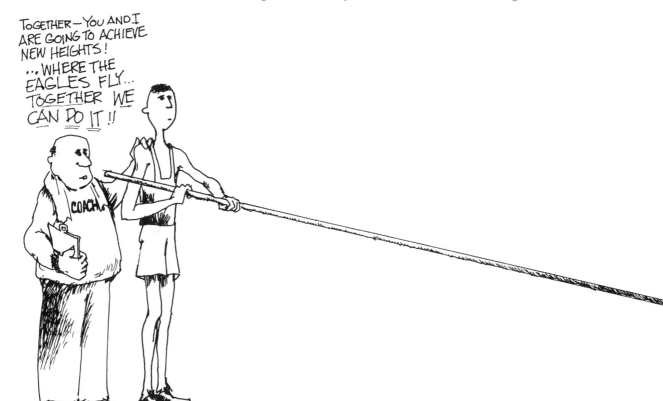

• identifying specific writing areas needing improvement based on present "writing status"

1. Identify the specific writing areas that need improvement

Managers can use our concepts of content, strategies, and language to define and prioritize specific writing areas that need improvement. The survey questionnaires can provide an initial framework for reviewing the researcher's present "writing status".[*]

Content: As the primary audience for researchers' documents, managers must specify what content areas need improvement.

Strategies: Managers should find out exactly how researchers go about their writing tasks and what percentage of time these tasks currently take. Then they can identify where writing procedures can be improved and productivity increased.

Language: The researcher's specific language problems should be defined.

---

[*] See pages 161 to 167 for copies of the survey questionnaires.

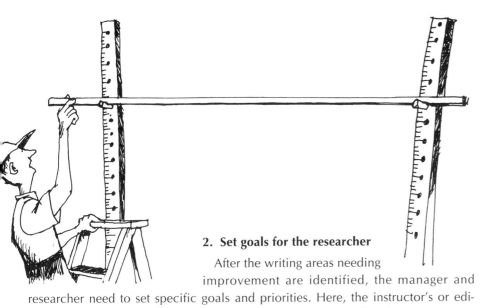

2. Set goals for the researcher

After the writing areas needing improvement are identified, the manager and researcher need to set specific goals and priorities. Here, the instructor's or editor's experience can help devise a balanced, achievable set of goals.

• setting realistic goals and priorities

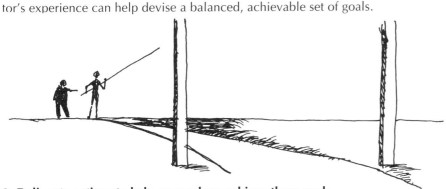

3. Delineate actions to help researchers achieve these goals

To help decide on the most effective actions, managers can review the chapters on *Steps researchers can take* and *Steps managers can take* (pages 15 and 77).

Then, after analyzing some of the researcher's documents, the instructor can help the manager and researcher map out the most useful and practical actions.

• defining actions that will lead to those goals

4. Decide on how to evaluate the researchers' improvement

This decision is extremely sensitive. As the prime readers, managers should be the main judge of content and readability. However, they should probably not be the sole judge of the researcher's improvement efforts: they may want to use pro-

• deciding on how to evaluate performance...

fessionals to evaluate progress in technical details of organization, efficiency strategies, and language. As one researcher commented:

> "Managers are often no more skilled at technical writing than researchers. Reviews by an experienced editor would be more helpful..."

...who will evaluate

If needed, other evaluators—e.g., project managers, peers, and "more distant" managers who need to use the documents researchers write—could be asked to review certain areas.

...and how much weight the review will carry.

Managers should also make researchers aware of how much weight the review will carry in their overall performance rating and what benefits researchers will gain from achieving their goals. For example, will a salary increase be proportional to improvement? Will a promotion require better—or even depend on—writing skills?

Here's an example of how a 1-year agreement was worked out for a researcher we'll call Jones (see page 101). In addition to a participating in a few proposals and an occasional journal article, Jones writes more than 12 research-related reports a year. The performance review focuses on these reports.

To be effective,

Obviously, this performance review procedure is neither easy nor fast. Managers initiating a review program may want to begin on a limited basis, see how it works, debug it, and gradually expand. For example, they might use it only with a few difficult cases at first.

Example: Performance review agreement

Step 1. Identify improvement areas

The manager and Jones used our "content, strategies, and language" approach to identify and prioritize the prime areas needing improvement.

Jones' reports had several **content** problems. Their organization was hard to grasp; conclusions, both technical and business, were usually omitted. Also, the reports were about 50 percent longer than the manager wanted.

Jones' writing **strategies** were time consuming: the reports were written by hand and then keyed in by a secretary on a computer. Jones had difficulty in finding large blocks of time to dedicate to writing tasks. All told, writing tasks occupied 35 to 40 percent of Jones' time.

Jones' **language** had two key difficulties: sentences were too long, and technical terms were rarely defined.

Step 2. Define goals

The manager and Jones agreed on the following 1-year goals—in order of priority:

- Learn the double-5 organizational scheme—and apply it immediately to the document in progress.
- Include a section called "Conclusions" in every report, even if the conclusions are still tentative.
- Shorten reports from their present 25 pages to 20 pages maximum. Ultimately, reduce the page count to 15.
- Try to reduce writing time to about 25 percent of Jones' total work time.
- Make sentences shorter (no more than 30 words) and more concise.
- Lessen the amount of jargon by spelling out all acronyms and defining technical terms.

Step 3. Delineate actions to achieve these goals

The actions the manager and Jones decided upon—with the advice of an instructor—were for Jones to:

- Undertake a "self-teaching" program, based on this book, to improve organizational skills. An instructor would be available to answer Jones' questions and to review the reorganization of the document now in the works.
- Attend an in-house technical/business writing course when it became available.
- Try to use the suggestions in this book for reducing document length and improving sentence structure; the instructor would help as needed.
- Preface each report with a note on improvements that had been attained for each goal.

The manager also undertook specific commitments to:

- Review all of Jones' outlines to make sure that only needed material is covered and that all organizational sections are included.
- Look into reducing the requirements for 12 research reports a year.
- Help Jones reduce writing time by reviewing schedules and initiating useful time management methods.
- Provide individual computers—or access to a LAN (Local Area Network)—for Jones' group within three months.
- Have the editor review the drafts of upcoming reports. The editor would coach Jones on how to organize the reports better and write shorter sentences. The editor would also point out jargon that Jones forgot to translate.
- Read the final reports to monitor Jones' overall improvement.
- Discuss Jones' progress formally at 3-month intervals.

Step 4. Evaluate progress

To fairly evaluate Jones' improvement efforts, the manager and Jones agreed that the manager would judge the final product's overall quality and usefulness, but that the instructor or editor would evaluate Jones' specific progress towards the agreed-upon writing goals.

The manager also explained clearly what benefits Jones would derive from making substantial progress toward these writing goals.

Two conclusions on performance reviews are clear. First, our survey showed that researchers are eager to "increase their ease of writing and reduce their writing time". They **want** to be more skillful, productive writers. Thus, for the performance review to be an effective incentive, researchers must perceive it more as an opportunity than a threat.

Second: numerous comments by both managers and researchers demonstrate that performance reviews have positive impacts only if managers provide the tools, backing, and encouragement to enable researchers to seriously conduct their improvement programs.

researchers must perceive these reviews positively—

and managers must provide the tools for researchers to achieve their writing improvement goals.

DO LIST FOR MANAGERS

Right away

☐ Learn the double-5 organizational scheme

☐ Provide precise guidelines **before** the writing stage.
Tell researchers...

- **Who** needs the document

- **How** the document will be **used**

- **What sections** of the double 5 organizational
scheme need emphasis

- **How long** the document should be

☐ Make guidelines clear and consistent

☐ Review the outlines of documents

☐ Give constructive feedback on content

☐ Help researchers plan uninterrupted writing schedules.

Start plans to

☐ Streamline writing requirements

☐ Make computers available, and encourage their use

☐ Hire a technical editor

☐ Delegate some of your review work to the editor

☐ Establish writing courses geared to technical/business needs

☐ Use performance reviews to improve researchers' writing

But

☐ Avoid massive editing: instead, indicate problem spots

☐ Delegate editing to editors.

CHAPTER IV

RESULTS TO EXPECT

RESULTS TO EXPECT

How these suggested steps will impact writing goals:
• Results from actions to upgrade...content...strategies...style   • Summary charts

Now you've seen what steps researchers and managers can take to upgrade technical/business writing. But you probably still have at least two key questions:

■ What results or benefits can I expect from investing in these suggested actions?

■ What rates of improvement and relative costs can I anticipate?

To give you an overall, realistic comparison of potential return on investment, we'll discuss the effects of actions to improve content, strategies, and style—especially language. Then we'll summarize the impacts of the steps managers and researchers can take on our three main goals of improving:

■ Document quality

■ Productivity

■ Writing skills

We'll also review or summarize the **rates of improvement** you can reasonably expect, and indicate the **relative cost or time** for implementing these steps. The summary charts on "Results to expect" (pages 110 to 111) reflect evaluations based on our experience and the survey responses.

Now let's look at results and benefits you can expect if these steps are taken...

at rates of improvement, and at relative costs.

Results from actions to upgrade...

...content...

The main technique researchers need to master is: organizing technical/business documents. Because the double-5 organizational scheme is flexible, and because researchers are already trained to adapt models to various needs, they usually learn to apply double-5 quickly. In fact, questionnaire results and feedback from our courses consistently show that both researchers in industry and university students rate double-5 highly and use it readily. Then, once it's an integral part of a researcher's arsenal, it vastly facilitates outlining, writing, revising, and analyzing documents.

Thus, as researchers' command of this technique grows, managers can expect to receive **logical** documents that are easier to follow and that contain the technical and business information they need.

A better **level of technical detail** should be evident right away and improvement should continue, **if** managers provide clear guidelines on what they need to know. Such guidance relieves researchers of time-consuming second guessing.

On the other hand, the ability to write shorter, more **concise documents** evolves slowly. Researchers have to get used to working with outlines, taking time to think through the ramifications and page estimates for each point. They must also learn

Mastery of the double-5 organizational scheme should steadily lead to more logical documents.

Precise guidelines from managers can quickly yield better targeted levels of technical detail.

With time, more concise documents will evolve and editing will become simpler.

to take a broader, more objective view of their outlines; to spot potential redundancies or unnecessary inputs; and to eliminate them at the outline stage as much as possible. This task is not easy: even experienced editors don't always succeed. But gradually, as researchers become more adept at thinking through and revising their outlines, their first drafts will become shorter and more concise. With time, the entire review and revision process will be simplified.

As clarity and focus also progress in tandem,

Improvements in document **clarity** and **focus** will parallel progress in the previously mentioned areas. Streamlining document requests and providing model outlines where possible will help improve focus.

overall content improvement will strongly enhance document quality and managers' understanding.

In our view, improvements in content will yield the greatest gains in **document quality**. Further, researchers who learn to plan and organize a document tailored to the needs of its readers will find they have gained a **skill** that automatically upgrades the quality of all their written work, improves their **productivity**, and increases their sense of satisfaction. Content improvement will also have the greatest impact on expediting managers' understanding of researchers' documents. Thus, efforts in this direction should receive top priority.

...strategies...

Improvements in several strategic elements can yield both productivity and quality gains—at varying rates.

Improvements in researchers' writing strategies can yield enormous productivity gains—but not all at the same rate. Some strategic elements will also favorably affect document quality. Here, we'll look at four elements—outlining and time planning, use of an editor, use of a computer, and better time management.

Tougher demands on outlines that:

Outlining and time planning. Developing **useful** outlines is a key skill for researchers to acquire. "Useful" outlines:

■ Help researchers work productively, with fewer iterations

■ Specify the kinds and extent of information to include

■ Reflect managers' (or other clients') information needs and guidelines.

These demands on an outline are tough to meet: they impose greater rigor and require more preparation time than researchers and managers may have expected; they often require manager's participation. The rate of improvement in developing such outlines will depend mainly on using the double-5 scheme successfully, and on delibarately allotting sufficient preparation time.

require honed organizational skills and adequate preparation time.

Realistically estimating time to produce quality documents requires basic changes in approach:

*Realistic **time estimating** requires a revamped approach:*

- ▣ Revaluating the ratio of time required per satisfactory document, both by researchers and managers
- ▣ Roughly budgeting adequate time for producing quality documents
- ▣ Adopting or adapting suggested methods to calculate this time more precisely when the outline is complete, but **before** work begins on the draft
- ▣ Reworking this estimate—and the outline, if necessary—until researchers and their managers agree on it, or until it can meet a required deadline.

Progress in both areas will probably be slow at first, but will accelerate with experience.

Progress, slow at first, will gradually accelerate.

As our example shows (pages 90 to 93), using an editor—especially **bringing a technical editor on board**—can probably yield the fastest return on investment. The right editor can immediately help researchers improve a document's organization and responsiveness to readers' needs. Largely on their own, editors can often vastly upgrade the style and readability of a document. They can relieve researchers of proofreading and production tasks. Thus, they offer researchers quick gains in productivity and document quality.

*Well planned use of **editorial help** can rapidly improve both researchers' and managers' productivity, and upgrade communication.*

But don't expect "dramatic" results all the time. Editors can't turn "sow's ears into silk purses". Researchers must learn to write well enough to convey their ideas. What editors can do is **improve** communications—to a degree. Only researchers can describe the frontier of science they have unraveled. Thus, if researchers write badly, an editor—with a lot of stamina, insight, and **time** for discussions—can **help** convert their work into a fair document. But, if researchers upgrade their skills and write reasonably well, an editor—with far less effort—can help convert their work into very good or even excellent documents.

But results will be tempered by:

• researchers' writing skills

Productivity gains from using an editor will depend largely on "operational" decisions. For example, if editors function as entrepreneurs, researchers often view editorial services as direct added costs to their projects. Except for a minority of "converts" who are convinced the editor saves them time, researchers are apt to restrict the use of such services to the later stages of document preparation—e.g., for minor language corrections and proofreading. And if the price for these services is high, many researchers will not use them at all. Thus, the potential productivity gains from this operational mode may be small.

• the work mode selected for the editor—and the costing method.

On the other hand, if editorial costs are built into the project's budget and the editor's function integrated optimally into all the document preparation stages, productivity gains can be high.

Managers' productivity can also benefit from using editors. In our example (page 90), the program manager spends only 5 to 10 percent of his time reviewing documents. The average indicated in our survey is more than 20 percent. This manager attributes much of his time savings to delegating review and revision tasks to the editor.

*Use of **personal computers** can yield dramatic productivity improvements...*

...depending on researchers' current experience.

But quality will improve only with upgraded writing skills.

*Better **time management** requires changes in work habits and strong management support.*

Though progress is apt to be gradual, it results in less interrupted writing, and more consistent, focused documents.

Computers can also yield substantial benefits quickly. But, while the potential productivity increase is enormous, the **rate** of productivity improvement will vary with the experience and adeptness of researchers in using the computer as a writing tool. For example, many recent university graduates are already comfortable with computer writing. They have used the computer to write project reports and theses, and are accustomed to highly productive writing and document production. Likewise, veteran researchers who use computers in their scientific work have adapted easily into writing via computer. Others who are new to this approach may adjust more slowly. However, our survey indicated that a large percentage of researchers could make quick gains in productivity by having a computer freely accessible for their writing tasks.

Between 1986 and 1993, computer use in industry jumped enormously. However, we have few exact figures on the extent of this growth for researchers' writing. Some anecdotal evidence and quantitative results suggest this increase varies greatly according to management attitude, company "culture", geographic area, and industry type. Another key factor is computer accessibility: the easier the access, the greater the use. Thus, researchers who have their own computer will use it more than those who need to "fight" for time on a department computer.

Though we have not measured the productivity improvement rate, several researchers commented that using computers reduces their writing time by 10 to 50 percent. This estimate may be conservative. One professor told us that computer use—with advanced word processing, graphics, equation software, and suitable printers—has improved the writing productivity of his students remarkably: what formerly took 4 to 6 months to complete can now be done in a little as 2 weeks![9] Another professor noted that in one company, researchers who did not have computers for writing asked their managers for a "handicap" in their performance reviews.[10] They claimed they could not possibly compete with researchers who used computers for writing.

On the other hand, computers do not automatically guarantee useful content, logical organization, or clear sentences. Improving writing quality by using computers also depends on upgrading writing skills. Further, learning to use computers optimally for writing is a skill that may need sharpening.

The fourth key strategic element—better **time management** to minimize interruptions and to maximize the use of time researchers dedicate to their writing tasks—is fundamental to increasing productivity. But initiating improvements in this area is more complex, probably because many ingrained work habits will need to change. Innovative solutions, strongly supported by managers, may have to be introduced. Thus, improvements will likely be gradual; but some may be dramatic.

For example, time savings achievable from uninterrupted writing and a quiet environment are hard to quantify. But the potential is huge because every unplanned interruption (and the survey indicates the frequency is high) causes a loss in writing efficiency. When writing momentum is disrupted, even for minutes let alone hours or days, researchers waste time reviewing where they stood; they must try to recapture their thoughts before they can continue. They don't always succeed. As one researchers commented, "You can't always write on demand".

Fewer interruptions also favorably affect document quality—especially consistency, continuity, and focus.

...and style—both language and format

Improving **sentence structure** is a long-term, incremental process. Certain parts are easier than others. For example, it's fairly easy to break up a long sentence into two shorter sentences; tougher to spot wordy, crutch phrases; and much tougher still to find acceptable alternative phraseology. Controlling the use of "and", prepositions, pronouns, adjectives, and "hedges" is even more difficult. But using parallel structure, minimizing passive voice use, and controlling jargon are probably the most troublesome areas researchers need to conquer.

The first step in improving sentence structure is to become aware of "good"—or "poor"—constructions or "language habits" that expedite or impede the reader's grasp. Obtaining this awareness requires experience and practice. Then, even with coaching, researchers may find it hard and time consuming to move from passive awareness to active revision. After all, they were trained to be scientists, not wordsmiths.

For these reasons, we've tried to focus on researchers' most common language patterns or "pitfalls"; then we've used examples to show researchers how to deal with these problems.

Thus, managers and researchers can expect gradual basic improvements—not professional smoothness—in sentence style and structure.

Word choice is an easier problem to alleviate. Managers should encourage the use of simple, direct, "unsophisticated" words. But it may be hard to convince researchers to stop using the stilted conventions some of them still equate with "scientific" language. We've already included a list of some of our pet peeves on page 59; you can add your own.

To solve the **jargon** problem, managers may need to meet researchers half-way.

(Continued on page 112)

Better language evolves slowly. Progress depends on:

• increasing awareness of good sentence structure

• shedding stilted conventions in word choice

Results to expect from researchers' actions

Actions by researchers	Rate of improve-ment	Potential impact on				Comments . . . and key factors for success
		Document quality	Produc-tivity	Writing skills	Cost or time	
Improving CONTENT	Slow–moderate	High	Med–high	High	Moderate	
Organization: learning and using the double-5 scheme	Slow–fast	High	High	Very high	Moderate	Proper instruction will speed improvement rate; better organization facilitates outlining and scheduling.
Level of technical detail	Moderate	Med	Med	High	Low–moderate	Managers' guidelines can increase improvement rate and productivity by reducing researchers' ''second guessing''; right level of detail simplifies use and grasp of document.
Conciseness and length	Slow–moderate	High	Low–med	High	High	May require additional time for more detailed outlining and revisions.
Logic	Slow–fast	High	High	High	Moderate	Almost insured **if** suggested organizational scheme is practiced; parallels rate of improvement in organization.
Clarity	Gradual	High	Low–med	High	Moderate–high	Will improve as a composite result of progress in above areas; learning to move from the general to the particular is basic to progress.
Improving STRATEGIES	Slow–fast	Med–high	High	High	Moderate–high	
Outlining and time planning	Slow–moderate	High	High	High	Moderate–high	Training in document organization and outlining can vastly increase improvement rate and can speed impact, especially on productivity.
Computer use	Moderate–fast	High	Very high	Very high	Moderate–high	Rate of improvement depends on present familiarity with computer use for writing; cost depends on amount of equipment already available.
Use of editors	Fast	Very high	Very high	Low–high	Low–moderate	Costs will decrease as researcher/editor interactions grow and as editors participate earlier in document development. Impact on writing skills depends on how much time the editor can spend on instructing researchers.
Time management	Variable; apt to be gradual	Med	Very high	High	Moderate	Rate of time management improvement depends on many site-specific habits and problems.
Quiet	Very fast	Med	High	Med	Moderate–high	Cost to provide private rooms where ''open-seating'' is now used will be high; cost to prevent interruptions may be low to moderate.
Improving STYLE	Slow–Moderate	Med–high	Low	Med	Moderate	
Sentence structure	Slow	High	Low	High	Moderate–high	Expect **incremental** improvements that enhance clarity and conciseness, not ''slick'' writing.
Word choice	Slow–moderate	Med	Med	Med	Moderate	Sensitivity to the need for better word choice may grow quickly; but ability to find better alternatives is apt to improve slowly.
Jargon use	Moderate	High	Low	Med	Low–moderate	Managers' pinpointing ''guilty'' words and acronyms can spur reduction of jargon.
Grasp and readability (mainly by formatting)	Slow–fast	Med–high	Low	Med	Low–moderate	Use of good design and modern computer technology can improve readability and help assure consistency—especially for documents with inputs from several sources.

Results to expect from managers' actions

Actions by managers	Rate of improve-ment	Potential impact on				Comments . . . and key factors for success
		Document quality	Produc-tivity	Writing skills	Cost or time	
Learning and using the organizational scheme	Moderate	High	High	Med	Low–Moderate	A key ingredient in helping guide, plan, and review researchers documents constructively.
Providing guidelines	Moderate	Med–high	High	Med–high	Moderate–high	Clear, consistent, complete guidelines are essential for upgrading productivity and document usefulness.
• Information planning	Moderate	High	High	High	High at first; gradually diminishing	Specific, well communicated guidelines can result in quicker improvements in **content.**
• Time planning	Slow–moderate	Med	High	Med	High at first; gradually diminishing	Managers' input and support are essential for researchers' progress in time management.
Reviewing document outlines	Moderate–fast	Med–high	High	Med	Moderate	Managers need to review **and** discuss outlines with researchers to assure complete and useful information, correct orientation, emphasis, and level of detail.
Providing feedback	Moderate–fast	Med–high	Med	Med	Moderate–high	Together with guidelines, review and feedback at critical points in document development can be converted to a **quality assurance** procedure. Additional costs depend on how much feedback managers now give. Feedback must be specific and constructive to increase improvement rate.
Hiring a resident editor	Fast	Very high	High	Low–high	Low–moderate	Hiring a resident editor for a line group can result in savings, not costs—both in time and funds. Impact on writing skills depends on editor's job assignments.
Streamlining writing requirements	Fast	Med–high	High	Moderate	Low–moderate	Front end cost in time to reevaluate, reduce, and simplify writing requirements; later, savings in writing costs. Minor costs to monitor and fine tune streamlining.
Making computers readily accessible	Moderate–fast	High	Very high	High	Moderate–high	High priority item; ROI can be quick. Hardware costs are decreasing.
Offering courses • Internal:	Slow–moderate	Low–med	Low–med	Low–med	Med–high	This expectation reflects the survey results.
Group + follow-up	Moderate	Med–high	Med	Med–high	Med–high	Assumes instructor continues interactive writing reviews with individual researchers to assure progress.
Individual	Moderate–high	Med–high	Med–high	High	High	Improvement requires firm schedules and well designed study programs based on individual's needs.
"Self-teaching"	Slow	Low–med	Low	Low–med	Low	Assumes "self-teaching" materials are relevant to technical/business writing. Rate of improvement and effectiveness can be improved by integrating "self-teaching" with periodic coaching.
• External: e.g., Universities	Slow–moderate	Variable	Low	Variable	Moderate	Impact will depend on course topics and design and on availability of follow-up.
Conducting performance reviews	Moderate–fast	Med	Med	Med–high	High	Rate of improvement depends on fair, constructive approach, reasonableness of goals, and support to achieve goals. One-on-one goal setting, monitoring, and interim reviews are time consuming. Impact could be high if salary increases are formally attached to performance review results.

• handling jargon more sensitively; managers can expedite progress if they:

▶

• facilitating readers' grasp through enhanced formatting—now accessible at reasonable cost.

Improvement in writing skills depends on type and frequency of instruction— and management encouragement.

Potential impacts of our suggested actions are summarized in the tables on pages 110 and 111.

But you can also expect synergistic results.

In fact, as editors see daily, researchers often have difficulty recognizing what jargon is! Managers can take three steps:

■ Circle jargon or any words they don't understand

■ Have researchers define those words (in a glossary if necessary), or replace them with simpler terms

■ Insist on having acronyms spelled out in full, especially when first used.

Managers can expect a fair pace of improvement in a researcher's sensitivity to jargon; nonetheless they must be ready to learn new terms that are a natural outgrowth of research discoveries.

Overall, however, researchers and managers need to remember that learning to edit your own document is much harder than editing another person's work.

To make major improvements in **facilitating readers' grasp** of regularly written documents—e.g., progress reports, final reports, proposals, manuals, evaluations—designers and editors can help establish standard, more digestible formats and "macros" that researchers, secretaries, word processing operators, and other staff can use readily. With the computers, software, and printers available today, researchers can produce documents with many readability-enhancing features that were formerly expensive and time consuming—e.g., two columns (instead of across-the-page typewriter format) with graphics and equations inserted as needed in the text, clear typeface, and various heading sizes. Thus, for a small investment of time and funds to interact with designers and editors, researchers will write—and managers will receive—documents that are far easier to read, scan, and grasp.

How fast researchers learn to integrate the double-5 organizational scheme, apply more comprehensive outlining techniques, and upgrade their writing style will depend largely on the training, instruction—and encouragement—they receive. If managers rely on researchers to instruct themselves—for example, by following the ideas in this book—the rate of progress will vary enormously, but will tend to be slow. Some people will be able to quickly apply many suggestions on their own; others will need help and time to practice. Overall, expect incremental progress at a rate of improvement roughly proportional to the amount of individual or class instruction.

Clearly, researchers and managers will need to invest time, as well as funds, to obtain worthwhile resutlts.

The summary tables on pages 110 and 111 compare the potential impacts you can expect from suggested actions. But, before using these yardsticks, bear in mind that:

■ Managers and researchers should expect **improvements** in researchers' writing skills—not magic conversions to professional quality writing.

■ The rate and extent of improvement will strongly depend on each researcher's talent, the time devoted to assimilating new skills, the type and amount of instruction, and the proactive support of each manager.

■ Increases in productivity will also depend heavily on ready access to resources and equipment.

However, as more of the suggested steps are implemented, you can aso expect synergies in the results that surpass the yields of each individual step. For example, just putting a computer on each researcher's desk is a giant step forward. Combining this step with effective use of a technical editor can yield dramatic improvements in quality and productivity, far greater than each step could provide alone. Further combining these two actions with more precise guidelines, streamlined writing requests, and well designed teaching can vastly escalate this synergy.

CHAPTER V

DEVELOPING WRITING IMPROVEMENT PROGRAMS FOR R&D ORGANIZATIONS

DEVELOPING WRITING IMPROVEMENT PROGRAMS FOR R&D ORGANIZATIONS

Top management must step in to strongly support and expedite "Writing Improvement Programs"—really "quality control programs"—that upgrade products and productivity.
• Preparing and implementing a Writing Improvement Program • Keys to success

So far, we've detailed researchers' problems in writing technical/business documents, looked at solutions both researchers and managers can implement, and discussed the expected results.

Up to this point, most of the discussion has dealt with steps **individual** researchers and managers can take. But some suggestions—such as establishing writing courses, streamlining writing requirements, or hiring and using an editor— require **organized group** actions, not just one-on-one remedial steps. Thus, we also need to focus on actions or programs to upgrade written R&D communications that can be undertaken by any size group—a large division, a medium size department, or a small section or company.

*Some of our suggestions require organized **group** actions.*

A coordinated "Writing Improvement Program" offers many benefits to groups. For example, it can:

A coordinated program can:

◄

- Reach and help all researchers and managers in the group, not just a subset of interested individuals
- Provide more cost effective planning and implementation—especially for high-cost items, e.g., purchasing computers or arranging writing courses
- Facilitate obtaining and coordinating optimum program inputs from various sources
- Eliminate duplication of effort
- Lead to more equitable methods for measuring results
- Yield clearer expectations of results at all levels.

Here, we particularly address upper management—executives who rely on written communications to decide on research directions, new product development, and funding. The reason: **to implement many of our suggestions successfully, especially large-scale writing improvement programs, strong policy support by top management is essential.** Without decisive backing and adequate budgets, writing improvement efforts will be severely hampered—and progress limited.

But, it requires strong support from top management.

Preparing and implementing a Writing Improvement Program

To upgrade writing skills, document quality, and writing productivity—our three goals—we suggest that companies use a six-step method to develop and implement a Writing Improvement Program.

We recommend a six-step approach to developing a Writing Improvement Program:

The steps are:

1. Conduct a "writing audit"
2. Determine the main writing problems
3. Define objectives for each writing goal
4. Plan a Writing Improvement Program
5. Implement the program and monitor its progress
6. Refine the program.

1. Conduct a "writing audit"

As the first step in developing an effective improvement plan, find out exactly what, where, and how pervasive the writing problems are. You need to know, for example:

1. Define writing problems by learning:

- How many documents researchers write each year
- How much time is spent on writing-related tasks—both by researchers and managers
- How much theses documents cost—including **all** staff time and other actual costs, not just researchers' time
- What writing problems researchers and managers identify and which of these are most troubling
- What strategies and procedures researchers currently use to write and produce their documents
- What solutions researchers and managers believe would work best—and why
- How successful these steps are proving.

Our survey questionnaires shown on pages 161 to 167 can be a starting point for listing items companies need to cover in this audit.

2. Determine the main writing problems

Analyze the audit results to identify the main problems and evaluate ongoing efforts. Then, prioritize the problems according to content, strategy, and language, as well as specific needs or "urgencies" within these categories.

2. Rank these problems according to content, strategies, and language.

3. Define objectives for each writing goal

Based on the audit analysis, define quantifiable and measurable group objectives and specify time frames to obtain improvements for each writing goal. For example:

Productivity improvement objectives

■ Reduce researchers' writing time by 5 percent of total time within 1 year

■ Reduce managers' reading-and-reviewing time by 10 percent of total time within 1.5 years

■ Reduce total writing costs by 10 percent within 2 years.

Quality improvement objectives

■ Improve document quality by 20 percent within 2 years. For example:

- On a scale of 1 to 10, increase content usefulness of written documents by 2 points within 1 year

- On a scale of 1 to 10, raise language readability by at least 1 point within a year, 2 points within 1.5 years.

Writing skill objectives

■ Increase researchers' writing skills, overall, by 10 percent within 2 years.

Measurement objectives

■ Within 3 months, develop workable criteria and methods to measure improvements and to track progress towards these objectives.

This final objective is easier said than done. Measuring improvement equitably implies:

■ Developing a baseline of current writing productivity, quality, and skills

■ Establishing criteria for measuring progress toward goals

■ Tracking improvements over specific time periods

■ Obtaining acceptance from researchers and managers.

The section on conducting performance reviews (pages 97 to 101) may provide some initial ideas for measuring or evaluating improvements. But they will need to be generalized, objectively quantified, and simplified before they can be broadly accepted and effectively used. Clearly, companies can expect to refine these criteria and measurement techniques as they gain experience.

These overall objectives will then become the basis for setting goals in individual performance reviews.

True, measuring improvements in content and writing skills may be difficult and time consuming, especially until readily applied techniques are established. However, for a writing improvement program to succeed, it must have sustained support; to obtain sustained support, it must yield measurable results—like any other improvement or productivity actions.

3. Define objectives for each writing goal and timeframes for their completion....

and develop measurement criteria and techniques.

4. Plan the program by assembling a task force that will:

4. Plan a Writing Improvement Program

Your writing improvement program should cover several elements: a schedule of actions, staff responsible for implementation, expected writing improvements, estimated implementation costs, anticipated savings in time and cost, and a budget. It should be prepared by a task force of managers, researchers, "auditors", and editors, who will need to:

▶ ■ List solutions to the identified problems. Review the suggestions in the chapters on *Steps researchers can take* and *Steps managers can take* (pages 15 and 77). If necessary, hold an idea generation session[4, 11, 12] to select or devise solutions, by adapting the suggestions here to specific needs, or by developing new options. Then check the "Results to expect" section and tables on pages 110 and 111 to see the potential impacts of these solutions.

Note that certain high-impact actions can yield improvements toward all three goals: document quality, productivity, and writing skills.

■ Estimate and compare the costs and benefits of the various solutions.

■ Based on the outcome of the previous two efforts, select the most effective methods to resolve the identified problems. The task force should:

• Look particularly for actions that contribute to more than one goal.

• For immediate implementation, tap those actions that only require shifts in **time** allocations for existing staff, not new outlays of funds. Such actions include:

— Self-teaching for researchers, according to the suggestions in Chapter II (pages 17 to 76), to improve content, writing strategies, and language.

— Implementing all the "immediate steps" managers can take, described in Chapter III (pages 79 to 83). These steps focus mainly on providing better guidelines, feedback, and time management.

• For longer term implementation, carefully weigh actions that require purchase, additional staff, or extensive coordination: streamlining, hiring editors, making computers available, establishing useful writing courses, and devising effective performance reviews.

Because the task force may find it cannot implement all the solutions simultaneously, it may have to decide on an implementation order. Such decisions will depend on the priorities established in Step 2 when the main writing problems were determined.

■ Develop implementation schedules, based on reasonable, achievable expectations.

■ Select staff responsible for implementation.

■ Develop budgets for implementing each facet of the plan.

Because several components in this program are crucial to its successful outcome—identifying the critical problems; selecting achievable solutions; correctly estimating the cost, time, and benefits of a suggested solution; and developing a reasonable implementation program and budget—companies may want to tap experienced staff or consultants who can help make optimal decisions.

5. Implement the program and monitor its progress

To make sure the program is operating effectively, appoint a standing committee to periodically measure progress, evaluate impacts, and solicit suggestions for conducting the program more effectively.

5. Implement the plan and appoint a committee to monitor its progress and evaluate impacts.

Some companies may prefer to implement their program first in a small group, watch the results, debug the plan, and only then transfer it to a division. Others may elect to use more sweeping solutions. For example: a large company did a detailed audit on writing-related time in one of its research groups. When the company found the average amount of researchers' time spent writing exceeded 35 percent, it convened a meeting of its division heads to discuss the problem and develop plans to resolve it.[10]

6. Refine the program

Because implementing a writing improvement program may be new, expect to modify it as work proceeds and results unfold.

6. Refine the plan as needed to improve its effectiveness.

Here are some key results from courses we developed for various companies. All these firms implemented several steps of our suggested program.

Here are some key results our courses yielded:

■ Usually, a "training task force" or "education committee" consisting of researchers, managers, and professional communicators initiated the course request.

■ The "writing audits" proved to be crucial in structuring courses to attack key problem areas.

■ Obtaining writing samples—e.g., reports, proposals, technical papers—from course attendees enabled us to pinpoint their specific needs, build the courses on actual writing tasks, and balance the limited instruction time most advantageously. Thus, each course was tailored to a particular group's goals and needs.

■ Instruction works best when two courses run in parallel: one for researchers, and one for managers. Managers and researchers must operate on the same wavelength for these courses to be maximally effective.

■ So far, improvements in writing quality and efficiency have not been monitored rigorously. However, in one case, several researchers suggested developing "writing quality standards"—similar to quality assurance measures in industrial production. The main proofs of success we see are "call-back" requests from companies to tailor a course for another group.

However, our experience with university students has shown that our content-organization model and editorial tools offer an excellent basis for developing equitable grading criteria and constructive improvement suggestions. These guidelines might be extended and adapted to meet company needs.

Keys to success

Thus, following these steps can indeed lead to a solid writing improvement program. But implementing it successfully depends on:

Successful implementation, based on :

- Obtaining cooperation—even enthusiasm—among researchers, line managers, executives, and instructors
- Securing commitment to invest funds and time, develop positive attitudes, take effective action, or purchase needed equipment.

...will lead to long-term improvements, but only through continuing efforts.

Management must also realize that the overall return on investment will be long term—though some improvements may be rapid. Further, as in other quality improvement programs, good returns will require continued efforts, not just a one-time shot.

CHAPTER VI

OUTLOOK: TRENDS IN IMPROVING RESEARCHERS' TECHNICAL/BUSINESS WRITING

OUTLOOK: TRENDS IN IMPROVING RESEARCHERS' TECHNICAL/BUSINESS WRITING

• A growing productivity thrust • Increased demand for quality documents • Expanded use of technology • Progressive growth in using editors • Adoption of a basic scheme for organizing documents • Streamlined writing requirements • Increased demand for useful writing courses for college students • Growth of in-house writing courses • Changes in the R&D manager's role • Changes in researchers' writing roles

---

At the outset of this book, we saw that companies seek excellence in researchers' technical/business written communications. Then, we saw how researchers and managers defined their problems with this type of writing. Through the rest of the book, we suggested practical solutions to these problems...and evaluated potential results.

While we have proposed solutions to the writing problems researchers and managers face...

But the obstacles to implementing writing improvements—by individual researchers and managers, or via programs for research groups—cannot be overlooked. For example, one manager wrote:

obstacles to their implementation remain.

> "It is sometimes hard to commit the time and money for writing-improvement programs because there are always high priority technical or research improvement courses and programs competing for the same money."

Clearly, the competition for staff time and financial resources is keen.

Still, two major drivers will spur companies to invest in actions to improve writing:

Major spurs to overcoming these obstacles are:

■ The huge amounts of time researchers spend writing—and managers spend reading—technical/business documents

■ The frequent failure of documents to adequately meet managers' or researchers' needs.

As companies come to grips with these problems, and try to help researchers produce better documents in less time, they will also see the need for enhancing researchers' writing skills to match the complex needs of industrial R&D.

To strengthen such efforts and put them into realistic perspective, we'll cover the trends we foresee in improving technical/business writing from a broad industrial R&D view. Based on the survey results, we'll also discuss the particular incentives—and barriers—to the appearance and growth of these trends. Further, we'll note changes that have occurred during the eight years since this book was first published.

We foresee certain trends in improving technical/business writing... together with incentives and barriers to their growth.

A growing productivity thrust

While companies already know the importance of written R&D communications, they may not have realized the enormous amounts of time and money expended on preparing various technical/business documents.

With Battelle's estimates and our survey results, companies can get a ballpark figure of writing-related costs for U.S. industry as a whole and for their own R&D groups. Let's review them quickly.

U.S. industry's cost for written R&D communications is very high...

Survey results show that researchers and managers spend an average of 28 percent of their time writing and reading such material.[*] Battelle projected that in 1993 U.S. industry would spend $83 billion on its own research, and would perform a total of $112.7 billion of research.[2] If we conservatively assume that 30 percent of that amount will be spent on researchers' and direct R&D managers' salaries, we find that their writing and reading of technical communications will cost U.S. industry $6.98 billion in 1993 (for its own research) or $9.47 billion (for all the research it performs)! This figure does not include the cost for top R&D management; nor does it include the cost for support staff—e.g., secretaries, word processing operators, and designers. Thus, the actual cost of R&D written communications is even higher.

and probably is high in your company too.

Now use these 28 and 30 percent assumptions to estimate your organization's writing costs. Remember that this figure is just a rough estimate: a careful writing audit may reveal an even higher number.[**] Then calculate the impact of a 5 percent reduction in time spent on written communications...

Such calculations will prompt many organizations to take urgent action. One company's response (described on page 119) is an example; another example appears on page 130. These organizations will aim both to trim expenses and to improve productivity by **reducing the amount of time researchers spend writing.** Savings can be used to conduct additional research, shorten development time for new products, purchase new R&D equipment, or improve profits.

Thus, many companies will take steps to reduce researchers' writing time.

To take effective actions, companies will also need audit information that shows exactly how much time is spent at each point in the writing process. Such audits are not easy to conduct: like other productivity audits, they must be carefully planned to assure acceptance and cooperation by both managers and researchers. Also, managers and researchers need to be prepared to make substantial—and sometimes radical—changes in their writing and reviewing procedures. In turn, these changes—e.g., widespread use of computers and professional editors—will demand major investments.

Growth of this trend depends on:

Thus, the growth of this trend will depend on :

- How aware companies are of this productivity problem—especially of actual writing costs
- How urgent this problem is for each company (i.e., the percent time now spent on writing-related tasks)
- How willing researchers and managers are to revamp currently used writing strategies and procedures
- How prepared managers and executives are to invest in the tools for increasing productivity.

[*] This figure is conservative; the actual percent may be considerably higher. See footnote on page 11.

[**] For example, recent audit results for researchers in two companies show the average amount of writing-related time is 35 percent, as compared to university researchers who average about 40 percent. However, in both contexts, writing time ranged up to 85 percent of researchers' work time!

Because of industry's intensive efforts to improve productivity, we are now seeing greater interest in improving the writing component.

Increased demand for quality documents

With increasing competitive pressures on research divisions to develop marketable products quickly, managers will start pressing for documents that are useful, logical, clear, and concise—the qualities they value most. They will also look for on-time communications that are relatively easy to read and understand. The reasons:

Demand for quality documents will increase because:

■ These communications are often the only R&D "products" that managers see for a long time

■ Quality, on-time documents enable managers to make better decisions, faster.

Researchers, too, want to produce quality documents that faithfully represent their creative, scientific work and conclusions. With clear directives, effective help, and better training, they will be able to write quality documents more efficiently—with less frustration.

Researchers need clear directives, effective help, and better training;

As in other quality control areas, companies may gradually realize that in writing, too, **early and continuous attention to quality results in better products at lower costs.**

but quality products mandate early, continued attention.

Some of the methods for measuring writing improvements will also be applied to assuring quality at critical points in a document's development. This approach merely extends the manufacturing principle of controlling quality during production rather than waiting to inspect the product at the end of the line.

Fortunately, several key steps to improve quality can be implemented without additional direct costs—e.g., managers' reviews of researchers' outlines; clear guidelines from managers that describe a document's required length, orientation, and emphasis; use of the double-5 organizational scheme to outline, write, and review documents; **early** time planning and outlining, with close cooperation between researchers and managers; and constructive feedback on document content from managers.

Though some quality "assurances" can be implemented without additional direct costs,

However, quantum enhancements of quality will again require substantial investments. Devising and implementing effective courses to improve researchers' writing skills—the foundation of better quality—will demand funding. So will streamlining document requirements to give researchers time for quality writing. But there are synergisms: the same computers and editors that increase productivity also upgrade quality.

...quantum enhancements require substantial investments.

Thus, the growth of this trend is a function of:

So continued quality improvement depends on:

■ Managers' and researchers' amenability and adaptability to this "preventive" quality control approach

■ Availability of—or willingness to invest in—computers, editors, streamlined document requirements, and custom-designed writing courses.

Again, industry's current emphasis on quality is fueling a growing demand for writing instruction.

Expanded use of technology

Increasingly, researchers and managers will use computers to upgrade writing productivity and quality.

Increasingly, researchers and managers will take advantage of computer-based technologies to enhance writing productivity and quality. Researchers' use of word processing will, we believe, become even more widespread within the next 2 to 5 years. But other computer applications are also available; and useful new hardware, systems, and software are constantly emerging. These technologies can exert profound changes on the writing process, both for researchers and for managers.

They'll also take advantage of useful, new technology: ▶

Here were our **1986** predictions:

■ With the growing trend in office automation, the use of **networked systems** and so-called **multi-user** systems will increase. Besides facilitating information sharing, such systems may reduce the cost per terminal for each researcher.

■ **Portable computers** (now called "laptops" and "notebooks"), compatible with standard office equipment and almost as powerful as their desktop counterparts, will be widely available and inexpensive. They could flexibly expand researchers' access to computers.

■ **Graphics** capabilities, already advanced, will be constantly upgraded and their use simplified.

■ **Printers** with enhanced design features will facilitate production of more readable documents at lower costs. Relatively inexpensive printers will mimic professional quality. In fact, "desktop publishing", including page layout, graphics, and extensive text printing options, will be a low-cost, quick alternative to conventional typesetting and printing.

■ **Text and graphics** of documents will be quickly convertible into slides for oral presentations.

■ **More accessible storage and retrieval capabilities**—e.g., using optical discs, and portable hard drives—will enable researchers to readily select portions of previously prepared text and graphics for use in current projects. Some researchers already use such techniques.

■ Wide use of **electronic communications**—e.g., electronic mail—will permit researchers to circulate documents quickly, even to distant offices. Then managers can use the documents electronically, manipulate document data, print out only what they need, and store the rest. With graphics already integrated, these electronic transfer procedures could decrease current document production time and costs. Use of such equipment will also speed up the interaction between managers and researchers. Easily integrated networks that link various computers will have to be available at reasonable cost, but will immensely facilitate information sharing.

■ **Voice actuated computers** for writing purposes could be a valuable tool; but they still require extensive additional development before they can be practical. When perfected, they will permit immediate printouts after dictation, without transcription by another person. Researchers who know how to dictate effectively will benefit most from these devices.

By 1994, networks, laptops, graphics programs attached to word processing software, laser printers, desktop publishing software, e-mail, and publicly available databases are already widely used. On-line communications—e.g., commer-

Helping researchers write...

cial on-line services, the Internet, in-house and commercial Bulletin Board Systems (BBS's) have gained broad, mainstream popularity. Advances in telecommunications technology have been exceedingly rapid, allowing very high rates of data transfer. For example, with fiber optic networks, we can send written, graphic, voice, and televised information rapidly, and "talk" in real time via computers. Research teams are gaining hitherto unprecedented abilities to interact even over large distances and to complete and submit their work remotely.

In addition, the proposal or report of the future may very likely be a CD-ROM.[*] The use of CD-ROM technology would be ideal for addressing a multi-tiered readership, since users can interactively select what level detail, or what consequence of the R&D, they wish to examine. An intuitive graphical interface, combined with graphics, animation, and sound, will vastly boost comprehension.

Strong competition in the hardware market and the rapid pace of development have resulted in declining equipment costs, especially for large orders. Thus, we can reasonably expect many companies to ultimately provide all their researchers with individual workstations, and to make other technological advances available.

As hardware costs plummet, more researchers will have their own workstations.

Certain software types or features particularly facilitate the production of quality documents. Here are just a few examples:

In addition to word processing, promising new software products include:

■ **Flowcharting software** enables researchers to map their ideas and graphically exhibit their trend of thought, allowing managers and clients rapid grasp of the researchers' goals and methods.

■ **The outlining capabilities of most word processors** permit researchers to insert, delete, move, collapse, or expand headings to any level and to print out a table of contents. Users can write the sections under the headings, then "hide" this filled-in section when they just want to view the outline.

■ **Spellcheckers** that help proofread and identify misspellings are already widely utilized. Because many allow words to be added, users can create a customized dictionary for their specialty. More advanced programs can identify some usage problems, and most recent word processors have a thesaurus to suggest alternative words.

■ Several **grammar checkers** that help identify and correct certain language problems are on the market. For example, a program may count the number of "ands", prepositions, and words in a sentence. Others may point to wordy constructions, suggest alternative wording, compute the "fog index"[**], or list the types of sentences used (e.g., simple, compound, complex). Some identify all passive voice constructions. However, companies need to be sure a grammar checker covers and matches their specific technical/business language needs. Unfortunately, so far grammar checkers are less effective and accurate than, say, spellcheckers, and they are not a substitute for researchers' language improvement efforts.

Today, newer word processing packages routinely include spellcheckers, grammar checkers, outliners, and thesauruses. Many also have graphics, oral presentation, spreadsheet, and extensive publishing capabilities.

---

[*] In fact, the Clinton administration in January 1994 made available a CD-ROM version of its 1994 federal budget.

[**] An index that determines the readability of a passage by calculating the number of years of schooling the reader would need to understand the passage easily.

Integrating these systems may require training and organizational change.

This rapidly developing technology, both hardware and software, can help researchers improve their writing skills, document quality, and productivity. Some can also help managers interact with researchers more effectively. Thus, companies should be alert to these new technologies and be ready to integrate useful products as they appear. At the same time, firms may have to make organizational adjustments and offer workshops to facilitate advantageous utilization of these products.

While our survey shows a trend toward using computers for writing,

According to our 1986 survey, some 30 percent of researchers said they used "computers with word processing";[*] 30 percent noted that having their own terminal would "help them most to improve their writing". Clearly, the trend toward using computers in writing was already under way. On the other hand, some researchers we worked with seemed surprised at our recommendation: they claimed, "I don't know how to touch type"; and some wondered, "What would my secretary do if I typed reports myself?" In 1994, the percentage using the computers as a main writing tool has undoubtedly grown. Best estimates are that between 67 to 80 percent of aerospace engineers in the U.S. use computers for writing—as well as for other information exchange and retrieval purposes. Figures in most other industrialized countries are lower.[13] However, we have not found data from a broad survey of researchers in the U.S. or elsewhere.

Many managers also were not convinced of the importance of using computers for writing: the 1986 survey showed that only about 18 percent of managers were willing to "provide researchers with more equipment and help—e.g., tape recorders, secretarial help, computer terminals". In 1994, the idea of using computers for writing as well as for technical tasks is much more accepted. In fact, many managers have already provided their researchers with computers.

growth will depend on:

▶

Thus, how quickly and widely these technologies will be fully integrated into the work flow of researchers' writing will depend on:

■ The cost of these new technologies

■ Availability of workstations for individual researchers

■ Researchers' adaptability to using computers for writing

■ The development of convenient networks for data transfer

■ Favorable attitudes by researchers and managers towards using computers for writing tasks

■ Availability of training and facilities to encourage computer use.

Progressive growth in using editors

To get a jump on improving quality and productivity, we foresee growth in the use of editors. Slowly, but increasingly, editors will become integral members of research teams or departments. Gradually, companies should also realize the advantage of exploiting the editor's contact with researchers to improve individual writing skills.

Editors will become integral members of research teams,

However, survey results show that only an average of 6 percent of researchers "ask for help from colleagues, managers or editors". So expanding researchers' use of editors significantly will require far-reaching changes in present attitudes

---

[*] This figure includes operator-run word processors. See further discussion on page 150.

and routines. Still, 22 percent (average) of researchers agreed they would benefit from "working with an experienced editor who can help pinpoint and resolve individual writing difficulties".

Further, survey results tell us that about 57 percent of managers "sometimes correct or edit—even completely rewrite" researchers' documents! Also, only 10 percent of Battelle managers and a mere 3 percent of B-TIP managers say they "**often** use an editor who understands their criteria to help researchers write better documents". According to researchers, this percentage is zero! (You can check these details on page 153.) In fact, "editing" may frequently be viewed as a research manager's function; courses are given and books are written for "the manager as editor".[14] So, the idea of a switch to using professional editors may be revolutionary, and may not always be readily accepted. On the other hand, as our example shows (pages 90 to 93), some managers recognize the potential time savings and quality increases; they are eager to delegate review and revision tasks to editors. The survey showed that, on average, 15 percent of managers are willing "to employ technical editors to assist researchers as needed".

Though editing is often viewed as a manager's function,

editors can relieve the manager of editing responsibilities

Increased use of professional editors could eliminate much of the editorial work that supervisors and managers currently do. Instead, managers could allocate more time to directing and guiding researchers on content, planning, and productivity issues.

Another potential difficulty in expanding this use: finding qualified professionals. To our knowledge, specific courses on technical/business editing are not widely offered. Companies may find they have to select candidates with skills in technical or science writing or editing, and train them on the job to orient communications to managers or other business constituencies. Alternatively, they may look for individuals with extensive business communications or journalism skills who also show potential for technical writing.

Another constraint: qualified technical/business editors may be hard to find.

Increased demand for editors' services will lead to more career opportunities...and a push for more university course offerings.

Because of these constraints, growth in the use of editors is apt to be slow over the near term. It will require favorable conditions for researchers to utilize editors...and a strong push from upper management. The cost/benefits are clear: professional editors can often work 30 to 70 percent faster than researchers, at 30 to 70 percent of the cost! In fact, some groups have already integrated editors or writers into their research groups. For example, at one of the U.S. National Laboratories, 40 or more people are working in a writer/editor capacity within the research groups. As a result, they save the scientists 25 to 75 percent of their writing time. Usually, the writers work directly with the researchers from a project's outset.[15]

Use of editors may be slow in the near term, but will accelerate as experience accumulates.

Thus, as more research groups succeed in dramatically improving quality and productivity via editors, demand for editors' services will increase—whether on an "as needed" or full-time basis. Then, "technical/business editing" may come to be viewed as a career path. Ultimately, universities and experienced consultants may start offering courses and training. In the long term, therefore, we anticipate substantial growth in integrating editors into the R&D writing process.

Adoption of a basic scheme for organizing documents

Adoption of the double-5 organizational scheme suggested in this book—or a similar unified organizational framework—will go a long way toward upgrading communications between researchers and managers. One researcher calls it "the expediting formula" because it facilitates interactions between researchers and managers in:

Adopting a unified organizational scheme—such as double-5—facilitates researcher- manager interaction in:

■ Planning and outlining documents

■ Spelling out what parts should be emphasized, downplayed, inserted, or omitted

■ Structuring—or restructuring—a document for different audiences and uses

■ Evaluating content

■ Preparing constructive critiques.

By improving guidance and feedback, this organizational scheme will play an important role in bridging the communications gap between researchers and managers that the survey so clearly revealed.

As researchers and managers see double-5's usefulness, its application will widen.

How rapidly will the double-5 scheme be integrated? The key question probably is: "When do you want to start?" Our experience suggests that, once researchers and managers grasp the idea and see how useful and flexible it is, they will quickly start applying it to more and more of their writing tasks. Feedback from industry researchers and university students confirms that double-5 has proven to be a valuable tool for planning, outlining, discussing, or evaluating a document. This scheme can also play a major role in the next trend we'll discuss.

Streamlined writing requirements

Streamlining will become a key tool for increasing productivity and quality. Internal "writing audits", with inputs from researchers, managers, and editors, will help pinpoint the types of documents where minimizing writing requirements will be most effective. Streamlining will also simplify writing tasks by focusing researchers' responses on managers' precise questions and needs. Such a policy, applied both to internal and external documents, will result in more useful communications written in less time.

Streamlining—carefully evaluating, restructuring, and reducing writing requirements—will be increasingly used, leading to better communications written in less time.

STILL A COUPLE OF ROUGH EDGES... BUT OVERALL — PRETTY SMOOTH !!

The double-5 organizational scheme will be used advantageously as a template for streamlining writing needs for different types of documents. It can prompt the "streamliners" to review the different kinds of information that might be needed.

Further, the **process of defining** exactly what purpose the document will serve, what information needs to be included, and how frequently that information is really required will alleviate two major problems researchers identified: deciding on the right level of technical detail and figuring out exactly what their managers want to know.

True, some managers can streamline writing requests for their individual programs. But, as we noted earlier (page 84), broad-based streamlining, especially for large groups, will require input and cooperation from various sources to be effective. Because it may result in changing many operational modes now taken for granted—especially in review processes that require almost interminable iterations—it demands open-mindedness to initiate, develop, and implement. Further, even after some streamlined methods have been introduced, the "streamliners" need to remain alert to new ideas for additional improvements. For example, with easily accessible electronic communications, managers' precise questions could be formulated as a computerized interactive questionnaire that asks researchers for the needed information.

But revamping writing requirements requires open-mindedness and cooperation throughout a group.

According to comments from survey respondents, several companies already have established "macros" or models for researchers to use. From information and organization viewpoints, these models greatly facilitate researchers' writing. However, they too should come under regular scrutiny to see if the amount of information, the frequency of reporting, and the number of reviews can be reduced.

Thus, the extent of streamlining that a company can introduce depends on :

The extent of streamlining will depend on:

■ The present status of implementing shortcuts to writing tasks

■ The willingness of managers and researchers to initiate major changes in their present writing forms and review processes

■ The operation of a task force (or other group) with authority to develop and implement streamlining.

Increased demand for useful writing courses for college students

As companies demand scientists and engineers with proven writing skills...

Both researchers and managers are voicing serious complaints about the writing education that scientists and engineers are now receiving. Managers are emphasizing that researchers must learn to communicate the results of their work just as they learn the scientific bases of their professions. One manager from the U.S. noted:

> "...The place to teach people how to write, and how to think and write, is in grades 1 to 12 and in college. I expect researchers to know how to express themselves. Having to teach them what I consider basic communication skills is an indictment of our educational system and its failure to teach what is important."

Another manager commented:

> "Since the career advancement and value to an organization of a researcher depends nearly as much on communication skill as on technical ability, why aren't proposal, report, and paper writing courses included in most Ph.D. programs?"

Only about a third of the researchers surveyed had taken university courses in technical writing; many questioned the effectiveness of these courses.

more universities will introduce mandatory technical/business writing courses.

Thus, we expect more companies to strongly encourage universities to require relevant technical/business writing courses in science and engineering curricula.

Some excellent programs have been established...

Some universities already have technical writing programs that include courses angled towards industry. MIT, for example, has a long-established "Writing Program" for undergraduate and graduate students that offers several technical writing courses oriented towards specialists, management, and the public. Of particular interest is their co-teaching program: engineering students' technical reports are graded by an engineering professor and a writing instructor. Stanford offers a course—also videotaped—on "Writing for the World of Work". The University of Washington even has a special department of Technical Communications situated in its College of Engineering. This well established department offers an excellent technical writing program for undergraduate engineering majors as well as courses for its own undergraduate and graduate degrees.[16] Several other universities also have well developed programs.

but overall, industry's needs are not being met.

However, current availability of such courses at U.S. universities is inadequate for industry's needs. Technical writing courses are often elective. Traditionally, they have dealt with writing for technical journals. Many universities do not offer any courses. Our 1988 survey of U.S. engineering schools' course bulletins showed that only about 30 percent included technical communications in their school-wide curricula.

This situation, however, may well change. Awareness of the need for technical/business writing courses is growing. Business-university interaction is increasing: for example, some companies are providing computers for student use and are cooperating to develop relevant "professional writing curricula".[17]

Companies should also advocate courses to train editors in technical/business communications.

In addition to encouraging universities to develop mandatory writing courses tailored to the real world of industry, companies should strongly advocate that universities train editors in technical/business communications. Such editors would fulfill a growing niche as companies seek to upgrade writing quality and productivity.

One way companies can have an immediate impact is to state clearly in their hiring policies for new graduates that they prefer or require candidates who have successfully completed coursework in technical/business communications.

However, even if many universities

■ Start offering courses in technical/business communications,

■ Begin making such courses mandatory,

■ Expand their current offerings, or

■ Develop courses to train editors,

companies may need to wait several years to reap the benefits.

But, even if universities act quickly, the returns will be long term.

Since 1986, a new factor has encouraged engineering schools to urgently add technical communications courses: ABET (the Accreditation Board for Engineering and Technology) has required engineering programs to demonstrate their students' competency in English communications—both written and oral. Because these programs must be re-accredited every six years, this requirement is a strong incentive for universities to introduce instruction in technical communications.

Growth of in-house writing courses

Because of:

■ The long time lag until universities broadly introduce—and companies benefit from—technical business writing courses, and

■ The urgent need for more productive writing,

companies will turn to in-house courses designed to meet their needs. For some firms, in-house courses may be the only route available to fill this training gap. In fact, some companies made this decision long ago.[18]

Which raises the need for in-house training.

Such courses offer several advantages. Companies retain more control: they can select the instructor, participants, content, format, goals, and time for the course. In-house courses may also be less time consuming for researchers.

Thus, we expect the investment in in-house courses to increase. In fact, in 1994, we are indeed witnessing such growth. (See also page 125.)

Because in-house courses offer advantages, their use should grow...

However, companies will also want to ensure an adequate return on this investment. Up till now, our survey shows overall results have been disappointing (see page 159). Thus, companies are likely to demand:

but only if they ensure adequate returns via:

■ Better, measurable results

■ New thrusts to make courses more relevant to the company's actual writing problems and document needs.

As techniques develop for measuring writing quality, productivity, and skills, researchers and managers will become more adept at monitoring and evaluating the results of such courses—and suggesting useful refinements.

Methods evolved for measuring writing improvements will also be used to monitor quality...

These measurement techniques will also be used to assess writing skills of prospective hires and to conduct more objective performance reviews.

and assess writing skills in hiring.

By 1994, we have noted limited progress in this direction. However, with increasing pressures on industry to document quality control procedures, some researchers and managers are looking for ways to define quality standards for their companies' documents. Our suggestion on page 119 offers a starting point.

Changes in the R&D manager's role

Managers will face a new challenge: helping researchers reduce writing time, yet improve document quality.

This task will demand their active participation on two levels:

■ **Content—What** information is included in a document

■ **Strategies—How** the document is actually written.

To help researchers write productively, **managers will participate more in determining content and strategies.**

Trends we foresee in the manager's changing role:

Such participation will also enable managers to help instructors design courses or workshops that reinforce the complex writing skills researchers need.

Here are the trends we expect to see:

Managers will help researchers by providing more effective guidance while documents are still in the planning stage. This "help interaction" will center on:

▶

- Outlining the contents of documents, including precise guidelines on information required for specific audiences, document length, and level of technical and business detail

- Realistically planning total time, schedules, and costs to complete a quality document, yet meet deadlines

- Planning the roles of editors, secretaries, designers, or other researchers.

...all present a new challenge to managers...

Of course, the degree of this participation will vary with different researchers and different documents. At times, it may simply consist of reviewing and approving a researcher's outline and plans. At other times, it may demand several iterations until a feasible outline and work plan are devised.

Managers will provide useful, constructive feedback on documents—especially on content, orientation, and overall readability. But they will stop functioning as "rewriters" or editors—or, at least, reduce the time they spend on such tasks.

Managers will make more effective staff, facilities, procedures, and equipment available to help researchers complete their writing tasks more efficiently. They will need to initiate and integrate several key support functions: editorial assistance, computer access, streamlining, and quiet offices or writing rooms.

which will change many of their tasks

Managers will encourage maximum use of these time-saving, quality improving methods. Many researchers won't need encouragement to use computers. But they may need to learn to use computers as an effective writing tool. Delegating writing and editorial tasks may require more encouragement.

Managers, too, will gradually delegate many of their current editorial tasks to editors. This shift will depend on changes in attitude and on confidence in the editor's grasp of the manager's requirements. One program manager commented that he spends only 10 percent of his time on writing related-tasks. He delegates the rest to the editor.

Managers will monitor progress more effectively. They won't concentrate on schedules; project leaders or editors can do that. But they will try to ensure that researchers' writing time is not interrupted; that controls are in place (via an editor or other means) to see that quality work is proceeding on target; and that the door is open to help solve problems as they arise—not at the end of the line.

Essentially, managers will establish a "writing support network"—including specifically designed courses—that researchers can readily access to improve their writing quality, productivity, and skills.

However, some of theses changes may not occur rapidly; the survey showed only about 24 percent of managers were willing to "put more time into working directly with researchers". Further, for some managers, gaining the knowledge to redirect their efforts, learning to give clear written and verbal guidelines, selecting feasible steps to take, and implementing them successfully will be a new challenge. While this book should help, many managers will benefit from workshops on, "How to Help Researchers Write Better Documents Faster". In fact, since 1986, both the author and Battelle specialists have developed and conducted courses for managers precisely on this topic.

These changes in managers' functions are summarized in the table on page 138.

yet reduce the time they spend on technical/business documents.

This new role will not demand more of the manager's time—although initiating these changes will require a concerted effort. But, if we look at a rough   esti-

How MANAGERS spend time on technical/business documents

NOW — 28 percent (or more) of total time

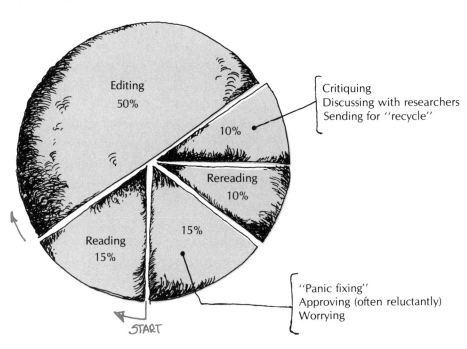

Editing
50%

Critiquing
Discussing with researchers
Sending for "recycle"

10%

Rereading
10%

15%

Reading
15%

START

"Panic fixing"
Approving (often reluctantly)
Worrying

IN THE FUTURE — 25 percent (or less) of total time

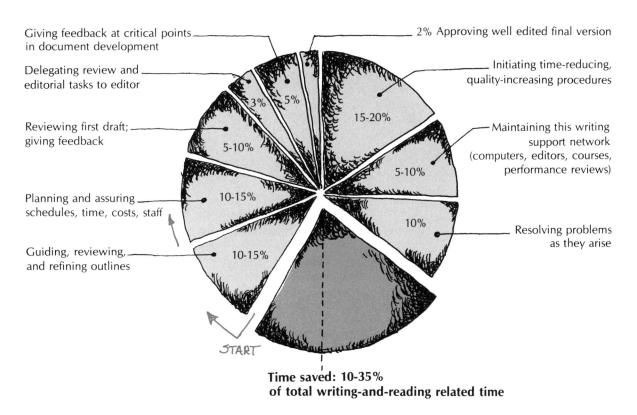

Giving feedback at critical points
in document development

Delegating review and
editorial tasks to editor

Reviewing first draft;
giving feedback

Planning and assuring
schedules, time, costs, staff

Guiding, reviewing,
and refining outlines

2% Approving well edited final version

Initiating time-reducing,
quality-increasing procedures

Maintaining this writing
support network
(computers, editors, courses,
performance reviews)

Resolving problems
as they arise

3%   5%

15-20%

5-10%

5-10%

10-15%

10%

10-15%

START

**Time saved: 10-35%
of total writing-and-reading related time**

The timing and extent of such changes will depend on:

▶

mate of how managers divide their writing-and-reading-related time now, and compare it to how they could divide their time in the future, we see a shift in tasks and emphasis, and a net **savings** in time (see charts on page 135).

Savings result from a drastic reduction in time spent reviewing and editing.[*] How quickly—and to what extent—these changes in line managers' functions occur will depend on :

- ■ Managers' readiness to work directly with researchers to provide better guidance and feedback
- ■ The severity of the writing problems in their R&D groups
- ■ The amount of time managers now spend editing
- ■ Managers' willingness to delegate tasks to editors
- ■ The encouragement and directives of top management
- ■ Managers' willingness to take on a new challenge

and, above all, on:

- ■ Managers' awareness of the cost for their current writing process—and the potential benefits of implementing productivity enhancing steps.

Changes in researchers' writing roles

Researchers will also focus on content and strategies as they change their modes of work and attitudes.

With increasing accessibility to effective writing supports, researchers will be able to improve their documents' quality and save substantial amounts of time. But taking maximum advantage of an emerging "support network" will also require deliberate changes in many researchers' modes of work and attitude. These changes will focus on:

- ■ **Content**—slanting document content to clearly defined user needs
- ■ **Strategies**—using new equipment, services, and approaches to save time and improve quality.

With work-oriented writing courses, researchers' writing skills will expand and improve.

To implement these changes, many researchers will need new skills to select and organize information for different readerships, and to utilize the "support network" optimally. When courses or workshops become available to provide these skills and to solve real writing problems, we believe researchers will want to attend. The survey shows that many researchers will welcome effective help to write quality documents more productively. Our work in industry since 1986 confirms this conclusion.

To integrate these changes and upgraded skills, researchers also will reshuffle tasks... and save time.

The trends we will likely see are shown in the table on page 138.

And the results? Again, as the conservative estimates in the diagrams at right illustrate, we will see a reshuffle of time expenditures, with a net gain in productivity and quality.

While time for outlining will increase, actual writing time should decrease dramatically!

This shift in writing procedures would add time spent on outlining and planning; the amount could reach 15 percent of the total allotted time. However, shifts to greater use of computers and editors would yield significant savings in researchers' total writing time. In our view, savings of 5 to 10 percent of researchers' total writing time are often readily attainable; in some cases, time savings of 20 to 30 percent are feasible. And on page 53, we show how savings of up to 45 percent of total writing time are possible. The example on page 130 documents an average writing-time reduction of 50 percent. In parallel, quality could improve 10 to 100 percent—depending on how you define "substantial" or "dramatic"!

---

[*] While our survey did not inquire into how much time managers spend editing, it revealed that about 57 percent of managers "sometimes correct or edit—or even completely rewrite" a document. Another study showed that direct supervisors spent 23 percent of their time editing, and 20 percent of their time writing. Managers spent 26 percent of their time editing and another 5 percent writing. See reference 1.

Helping researchers write...

How RESEARCHERS spend time on technical/business documents

NOW — 28 percent (or more) of total time

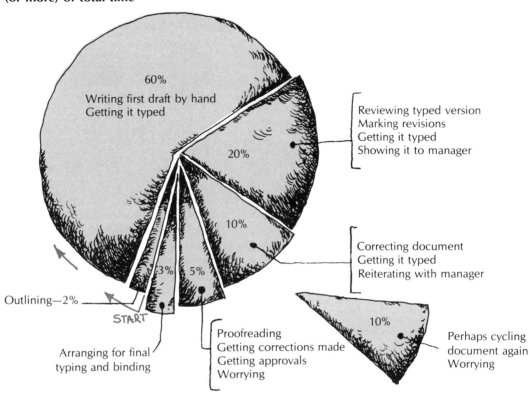

60%

Writing first draft by hand
Getting it typed

20%

Reviewing typed version
Marking revisions
Getting it typed
Showing it to manager

10%

Correcting document
Getting it typed
Reiterating with manager

Outlining—2%

START

3%

5%

10%

Perhaps cycling
document again
Worrying

Arranging for final
typing and binding

Proofreading
Getting corrections made
Getting approvals
Worrying

IN THE FUTURE — 25 percent (or less) of total time

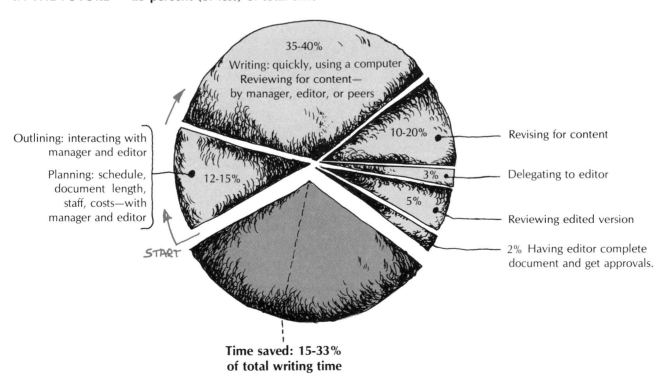

35-40%

Writing: quickly, using a computer
Reviewing for content—
by manager, editor, or peers

10-20%

Revising for content

Outlining: interacting with
manager and editor

Planning: schedule,
document length,
staff, costs—with
manager and editor

12-15%

3%

Delegating to editor

5%

Reviewing edited version

2% Having editor complete
document and get approvals.

START

**Time saved: 15-33%
of total writing time**

As these trends emerge, continued improvements will follow. And, as researchers and managers see these results and gain experience in upgrading written products, new approaches to enhance technical/business writing will appear.

Finally, we confidently predict: If researchers and managers use their famed innovative drive to foster writing improvements, researchers will more efficiently produce better quality documents...that managers can better understand and use.

RESEARCHERS AND MANAGERS WILL FACE A NEW CHALLENGE
Reducing writing time...yet improving quality

Changes in managers' role	Changes in researchers' role
■ Give more guidance on **content,** in the outline stage	■ Tune in more to a company's (or client's) business as well as technical needs
■ Streamline outlines and models wherever possible	■ Increase time spent on outlining to specify content
■ Participate actively in planning the writing procedure and schedule, especially for long documents	■ Plan schedules and costs realistically to meet quality, time, and budget constraints
■ Introduce time-saving methods—e.g., using computers, editors, good time management practices—and encourage their maximal use	■ Plan effective utilization of writing time
■ Make time-saving services and equipment **easily** accessible	■ Interact and iterate with the manager at the planning stage to obtain agreement on content, total time, schedules, and key review points
■ Provide constructive feedback on content and readability, at key points **during** the writing process	■ Discuss any problems with the managers **as they arise,** not after the document is completed
■ Protect researchers' planned writing time	■ Learn to use the computer for writing efficiently
■ Assure quiet space	■ Write first draft and revise for content
■ Be available to resolve problems promptly as they arise	■ Delegate work to editors and others as early as possible in the writing process
■ Introduce results-oriented courses or workshops to fill identified needs.	■ Take advantage of specially designed courses or workshops to upgrade needed writing skills.
BUT:	*BUT:*
■ Stop functioning as an editor or re-writer	■ Vastly reduce large scale editing, proofreading, and production activities
■ Delegate editing and schedule-adherence tasks to others.	■ Drastically cut writing with pencil and paper.
	In short, take advantage of the "writing support network".

CHAPTER VII

SURVEY RESULTS AND INTERPRETATION

SURVEY RESULTS
AND INTERPRETATION*

Result highlights that underlie this book's thrust appear on pages 8 and 9. Here we discuss the details.

To obtain representative and meaningful results, we organized our survey to cover a broad range of researchers and managers, both among B-TIP members worldwide and at Battelle. Our aim was to elicit specific, easily quantified replies to each question. Also, we enabled and encouraged respondents to qualify their answers and express their opinions. As a whole, the questionnaires to managers and researchers were not identical; but several questions were identical or similar. The rest covered issues specific to each group. Copies of the questionnaires appear on pages 161 to 167.

The questionnaires were sent to researchers and managers at B-TIP member companies and at Battelle-Columbus. Among B-TIP members—155 firms worldwide at the time of the survey—70 companies responded, usually through several researchers and managers. At Battelle, 45 percent of those polled replied. A total of 1307 replies came from:

- 520 researchers at B-TIP member companies

- 274 researchers at Battelle

- 421 managers at B-TIP member companies

- 92 managers at Battelle.

For the purposes of this book, we wanted to see the main trends in responses. Therefore, we calculated the percentage of respondents replying to each item in each question, and ranked the results according to these percentages. (Not surprisingly, the percentages do not always add up to 100.) Our evaluations of the results are based on the complete set of numerical data and comments obtained both from B-TIP members and from Battelle staff.

While all the researchers' and managers' comments are too numerous to be included in this chapter, their flavor is sprinkled throughout the book. The ranked numerical results are summarized in the upcoming tables. To help readers follow our discussion more easily, interpretations of the results appear together with the

---

* Survey questionnaires on "Helping Researchers Write...So Managers Can Understand" were mailed in October 1984. Results were received, tabulated, and analyzed by February 1985.

tables. The numbers beside each survey question correspond to those in the questionnaire—e.g.,

R 1 = Researchers' question 1

M1 = Managers' question 1.

Throughout this discussion, bear in mind that we are dealing with four groups of respondents:

Researchers • from B-TIP member companies

     • from Battelle

Managers • from B-TIP member companies

     • from Battelle.

For short, we'll call them "B-TIP researchers and managers" and "Battelle researchers and managers". The replies from B-TIP researchers formed the basis for ordering the rankings.

The few differences in the results from companies and from Battelle stem mainly from Battelle's specific business: providing a broad range of R&D services to industry and government. However, managers' rankings across the board—especially of researchers' writing problems and efforts to resolve them—were very similar. Researchers' rankings of results also showed strong similarities. The main differences arose in researchers' and managers' perceptions of efforts under way to help researchers improve their writing.

Types of documents most frequently written or read (R1, M1)

All four groups of respondents agreed on the type of document they deal with most frequently: reports on research projects. Next, in the list for B-TIP respondents came memos and proposals. At Battelle, proposals assume relatively greater importance than at B-TIP companies: 84 percent of Battelle researchers (vs 34 percent of B-TIP researchers) and 92 percent of Battelle managers (vs 36 percent of B-TIP managers) named proposals as major documents they write or review. At B-TIP companies, on the other hand, more researchers write (and managers read) requests and plans for funding new technology development.

Also of interest: 27 percent of B-TIP researchers and 53 percent of Battelle researchers write technical articles for scientific journals. Similarly, 23 percent of B-TIP managers and 38 percent of Battelle managers review such articles.

Researchers / **Managers**

Percent B-TIP	Percent Battelle	Rank B-TIP	Rank Battelle	Types of documents most frequently written or read	Percent B-TIP	Percent Battelle	Rank B-TIP	Rank Battelle
85	93	1	1	Reports on research projects	85	96	1	1
69	55	2	3	Memos	62	45	2	3
34	84	3	2	Proposals	36	92	3	2
27	53	4	4	Technical articles for scientific journals or conferences	23	38	6	4
19	6	5	8	Plans and budgets for technology development in your R&D group	26	15	5	6
17	13	6	5	Requests for funding new product or new technology development	27	18	4	5
14	9	7	6	Technical communications for non-specialists (e.g. company staff, shareholders, or general public)	12	9	8	8
8	7	8	7	Technical evaluations of proposed R&D investments	22	15	7	6

Several B-TIP researchers mentioned that they write operation manuals and documentation for users of their new products. They also listed patent applications, correspondence with outside vendors, technical monitoring reports on outside development, and engineering policies and procedures.

However, as one B-TIP manager commented,

> "Research reports are the most time consuming to write and the most difficult to read".

Amount of time spent writing or reading these research-related documents (R2, M2)

This is an eye-opener. As the table shows, approximately half of the researchers and managers surveyed spend 20 to 40 percent of their time writing or reading documents. And some spend even more time on such activities.*

Time, percent	B-TIP researchers	B-TIP managers	Battelle researchers	Battelle managers
0-20	42	43	18	39
21-40	42	45	50	52
41-60	12	10	20	8
61-80		1	8	1
81-100			1	

Such results lead to crucial questions about R&D cost benefits and productivity:

■ Are R&D organizations aware that such large amounts of time are spent on written communications?

■ Are such expenditures of time justified?

■ Are researchers properly equipped and trained for such writing tasks?

■ If not, how does this deficiency impact the cost benefits R&D organizations obtain from their staffs?

■ What steps can R&D organizations take—can researchers and managers take—to increase the ratio of research-to-writing time, yet upgrade the quality of researchers' writing?

Key qualities that technical/business documents should have (R3, M3)

All respondents strongly agreed that these qualities are:

■ Clarity

■ Easily read technical explanations

■ Conciseness

■ Logical, easily grasped organization

■ Relevant, accurate information.

* In fact, if we take into account the well-documented tendency to underestimate the amount of time spent on a task, this figure could actually be much higher. Note that a detailed study for one company's R&D division, conducted by MIT, concluded that an average of 35 percent of researchers' and their supervisors' time was spent on writing-related tasks. See reference 1.

While B-TIP managers and researchers ranked ''logical organization'' in fourth and fifth place, Battelle researchers and managers ranked this quality in second place.

Researchers				**Key qualities technical/business documents should have**	**Managers**			
Percent		Rank			Percent		Rank	
B-TIP	Battelle	B-TIP	Battelle		B-TIP	Battelle	B-TIP	Battelle
71	82	1	1	Clear, unambiguous writing	74	84	1	1
66	66	2	2	Easily read and understood technical explanations	58	64	2	3
65	58	3	4	Conciseness	55	59	3	4
48	46	4	5	Relevant, accurate information in response to requests	38	39	5	6
47	66	5	2	Easily grasped, logical organization	49	69	4	2
27	25	6	7	Useful information on business impacts of the technology	32	23	6	7
25	37	7	6	Correct grammar and almost-error-free spelling	23	41	7	5
3	4	8	8	Compliance with required format	5	14	8	8

Why are researchers' written documents important in your company? (R4, M4)

In B-TIP companies, written documents are used mainly to:

■ Communicate R&D results throughout the company (72 percent of both researchers and managers)

■ Decide on R&D directions and investments (53 percent of researchers and managers)

■ Identify and evaluate new product concepts (37 percent of researchers, 41 percent of managers).

However, these actions may take place in several stages; and some documents may have several groups of readers. In answer to the question, **''Who are the primary readers of documents you write?''** (a question in the personal history part of the survey not described here), researchers overwhelmingly ranked their direct

Researchers				**Why are researchers' written documents important in your company?**	**Managers**			
Percent		Rank			Percent		Rank	
B-TIP	Battelle	B-TIP	Battelle		B-TIP	Battelle	B-TIP	Battelle
73	39	1	2	Communicate R&D results throughout the company	71	43	1	2
52	29	2	3	Decide on R&D directions and investments	53	33	2	3
37	19	3	6	Identify and evaluate new product concepts	41	11	3	7
30	21	4	5	Prevent decisions based on vague or undocumented information	34	22	4	5
28	28	5	4	Stimulate and synergize new ideas	31	28	5	4
15	18	6	7	Advance researchers' careers	11	14	7	6
12	11	7	8	Boost R&D productivity	15	9	6	8
6	67	8	1	Obtain clients for contract research	6	89	8	1

R&D group managers first (67 percent), project managers and other researchers second (48 and 47 percent respectively), and then executives in top management (23 percent). Thus, one of the primary purposes of written R&D documents is **to monitor research progress.**

The two next ranked reasons B-TIP respondents gave for the importance of written communications were:

■ To prevent decisions based on vague or undocumented information (30 percent researchers, 34 percent managers)

■ To stimulate and synergize new ideas (28 percent researchers, 31 percent managers).

Several managers commented that written documents were used in their companies "for all the above reasons and **to avoid reinventing the wheel";** also **"to avoid duplication of effort".** However, one manager may have summed it up best: written materials are important...

> "...to assure adequate progress is continuing on funded work... to make sure that problems surface and that decisions are rendered quickly".

Researchers agreed. But they also noted that written documents help protect proprietary materials and patents, and signal guideposts for future work. Written documents are also important, they claimed, to identify unforeseen problems, demonstrate an R&D group's productivity, and establish and communicate common criteria for new product development.

Both researchers and managers at Battelle emphasized in their comments that written documents—especially research reports—"are Battelle's main product"; they are the vehicle for "communicating R&D results to clients".

Numerical results showed that written communications also are important for the organization

■ To obtain clients for contract research (researchers 67 percent, managers 89 percent)

■ To communicate results throughout the company (researchers 39 percent, managers 43 percent)

■ To decide on R&D directions and investments (researchers 29 percent, managers 33 percent).

These results corroborate those of question 1: proposals emerged as the type of writing most Battelle managers need to read, and as the second ranked type researchers need to write.

With this background in mind, we now can ask:

What are the **main writing problems** that researchers and managers encounter?

We'll highlight the main writing problems based on our "loose categorization" in the questionnaire. For researchers, this classification included **content, mechanics,** and **writing procedures.** For managers, it included **content, mechanics,** and **style.***

---

* The term "loose categorization" is used intentionally: the mechanics section for researchers, in fact, includes some elements of style.

Problems in content

Managers' view (M5)

B-TIP and Battelle managers agreed on four major content problems—but ranked them differently:

■ Information is difficult to scan and grasp quickly (49 percent B-TIP: 46 percent Battelle)

■ Poor or cumbersome organization (35 percent B-TIP; 55 percent Battelle)

■ Logic leading to conclusions is unclear, unconvincing, or lacking (35 percent B-TIP; 46 percent Battelle)

■ Conclusions and recommendations not spelled out in business terms (27 percent B-TIP; 34 percent Battelle).

Note particularly that "poor or cumbersome organization" is the highest ranked problem at Battelle; it also received the largest overall percent of responses in this question.

A fifth element—"extraneous and irrelevant material included; not responsive to requests for information"—also was marked by 34 percent of Battelle managers, but only 25 percent of B-TIP managers. B-TIP managers (27 percent) were more concerned than Battelle managers (19 percent) that "the impacts of technological advances on the company's business needs, problems, and goals are inadequately addressed".

Problems in content	Managers			
	Percent		Rank	
	B-TIP	Battelle	B-TIP	Battelle
Information is difficult to scan and grasp quickly	49	46	1	2
Poor or cumbersome organization	35	55	2	1
Logic leading to conclusions is unclear, unconvincing, or lacking	35	46	2	2
Conclusions and recommendations not spelled out in business terms	27	34	4	4
Impacts of technological advances on the company's business needs, problems, and goals are inadequately addressed	27	19	4	8
Extraneous and irrelevent material included; not responsive to requests for information	25	34	6	4
Too much technical detail	22	31	7	6
Explanations of general technological concepts are unclear	18	23	8	7

Researchers' view (R5)

B-TIP and Battelle researchers also agreed on the four top-ranked content problems:

■ Deciding what technical information and level of detail to include (58 percent B-TIP researchers, 60 percent Battelle researchers)

■ Making sure the logic leading to conclusions is clear and convincing, with no gaps (33 percent B-TIP, 38 percent Battelle)

■ Organizing the document to facilitate reading and grasp (33 percent B-TIP researchers, 36 percent Battelle researchers)

■ Figuring out what the manager (or information requester) really wants to know (28 percent B-TIP, 27 percent Battelle).

Thus, an interesting point emerged: though researchers found "deciding on what technical information and level of detail to include" most difficult, managers gave lower priority to the two related problems in this area—"too much technical detail", and "unclear explanations of general technological concepts".

Researchers

Percent		Rank		Problems in content
B-TIP	**Battelle**	**B-TIP**	**Battelle**	
58	60	1	1	Deciding what technical information and level of detail to include
33	38	2	2	Making sure the logic leading to conclusions is clear, convincing, and without gaps
33	36	2	3	Organizing the document to facilitate reading and grasp
28	27	4	4	Figuring out what the manager or the information requester really wants to know
24	21	5	5	Simplifying descriptions of technical problems and concepts for non-specialist managers
11	18	6	6	Writing transitions from one point to another
9	5	7	7	Developing and including the requested business information

Problems in mechanics

Managers' view (M6)

As the table shows, B-TIP and Battelle managers ranked all six problems here in exactly the same order. The top three problems are:

■ Poor sentence construction

■ Too much jargon

■ Imprecise word choice.

Notice particularly the sharp breaks in score between the top, the next two, and the bottom three problems. These results, bolstered by many managers comments, are extremely instructive.

Problems in mechanics	Managers			
	Percent		Rank	
	B-TIP	**Battelle**	**B-TIP**	**Battelle**
Poor sentence construction (e.g., sentences are too long, awkward, or similar in form)	68	79	1	1
Too much jargon; many undefined technical terms	43	43	2	2
Imprecise word choice	24	38	3	3
Faulty grammar	17	20	4	4
Spelling errors	15	17	5	5
Improper punctuation	6	11	6	6

Researchers' view (R6)

B-TIP and Battelle researchers also ranked problems in mechanics similarly. By far, the largest percentages of researchers in both groups agreed that the main problems are sentence structure and word choice. However, researchers barely recognized "jargon" as a problem, whereas managers ranked it as the second most serious problem—a major difference in perception. On the other hand, researchers agreed with managers that problems in spelling, grammar, and punctuation are far less severe.

Researchers

Percent		Rank		Problems in mechanics
B-TIP	**Battelle**	**B-TIP**	**Battelle**	
59	47	1	1	Structuring sentences so they are easy to read
47	45	2	2	Choosing the exact words
11	12	3	3	Avoiding jargon
11	12	3	3	Spelling
9	10	5	5	Punctuating correctly
8	9	6	6	Producing documents of the prescribed length
8	6	6	8	Following requested formats
6	9	8	6	Using correct grammar

Problems in style (M7)

As a separate section, detailed questions on **style** were only put to managers. However, three items in the researchers' question on **mechanics** also dealt with style: sentence structure, use of jargon, and word choice.

For managers, two important problems stand out:

■ Documents are hard to read; their focus and meaning is unclear (63 percent average)

■ They are too long; not concise (45 percent B-TIP; 41 percent Battelle).

Also, the item "documents are cluttered or overly elaborate" was marked by 22 percent of B-TIP managers and 25 percent of Battelle managers. If we combine this result with the document length issue, the problem of overly long documents assumes even more importance.

Here again, the perceptions of researchers and managers differed widely. While an average of 43 percent of managers from both groups indicated document length as a serious issue, only 9 percent of researchers said they had a problem in "producing documents of prescribed length."*

Note that Battelle managers placed greater emphasis on smooth transitions and on following requested formats than did B-TIP managers. Also, more Battelle managers are concerned about variations of inputs from different researchers. Again, these differences probably reflect Battelle's need to produce quality, multi-authored documents for external clients.

---

* For convenience, these are "straight", unweighted averages, even though the B-TIP group of managers is 4.6 times as large as the Battelle group, and the B-TIP researchers' group is 1.9 times as large as the Battelle group.

Helping researchers write...

Problems in style	Managers			
	Percent		Rank	
	B-TIP	Battelle	B-TIP	Battelle
Hard to read and understand; focus and meaning unclear	62	63	1	1
Too long; not concise	45	41	2	2
Great variation of input from DIFFERENT researchers	26	40	3	3
Poor transitions; writing leaps from one point to another	23	34	4	4
Cluttered; overly elaborate	22	25	5	5
Not persuasive	15	20	6	6
Requested format not followed	7	13	7	7
Variation in quality of writing from the SAME researcher	3	4	8	8

Problems in writing procedures (R7)

The questions in this section only applied to researchers. The results revealed that the top two ranked problems were the same for B-TIP and Battelle researchers:

1. Finding large enough chunks of time to write efficiently (48 percent B-TIP; 46 percent Battelle)
2. Getting started (45 percent B-TIP and Battelle)

Three other problems were also stressed, especially by Battelle researchers.

■ Writing the first draft (29 percent B-TIP; 25 percent Battelle)

■ Producing quality writing within allotted budgets (29 percent Battelle; 8 percent B-TIP)

■ Meeting short, frequent deadlines (21 percent Battelle; 13 percent B-TIP).

Such results indicate that improvements are urgently needed not only in writing procedures *per se,* but in time management and workload allocation.

Only about 19 percent of researchers listed "preparing a useful outline" as a problem. Yet, managers' main complaint is that documents are long, hard to read, and difficult to grasp. Because the outline is the root from which the final product grows, and most researchers claim they follow their outlines reasonably well (see results of question R9), researchers may have a bigger outlining problem than they realize.

Researchers				Problems in writing procedures
Percent		Rank		
B-TIP	Battelle	B-TIP	Battelle	
48	46	1	1	Finding large enough chunks of time to write efficiently
45	45	2	2	Getting started
29	25	3	4	Writing the first draft
20	17	4	6	Preparing a useful outline or plan
13	21	5	5	Meeting short, frequent deadlines
13	15	5	7	Revising and editing your own draft
8	29	7	3	Producing quality writing within allotted budgets
2	5	8	8	Sticking to the outline

Writing tools and surroundings (R8, M8)

Despite the much heralded advent of the "computer age", 90 percent of researchers still use pencil and paper as their principal writing tools! Though 54 percent of managers claim that personal computers or word processing terminals are available for researchers' use, only about 30 percent of researchers say they use these tools. Many respondents indicated that "available" terminals are often group-used word processors with special operators. Several researchers commented that one PC was "available" for 20 researchers; others noted that use of computers for writing was discouraged—or even off limits—for scientists and engineers. One manager stated, "... secretaries and typing are available. Therefore, personal word processing is not needed." But another manager claimed that "... researchers seem reluctant to use anything but pencil and paper."

Researchers / Writing tools and surroundings / Managers

Percent B-TIP	Percent Battelle	Rank B-TIP	Rank Battelle	Writing tools and surroundings	Percent B-TIP	Percent Battelle	Rank B-TIP	Rank Battelle
90	90	1	1	Pencil and paper	84	91	1	1
29	32	2	2	Computer with word processing	54	54	2	4
				Private, quiet office	41	85	3	2
6	12	3	3	Tape recorder	37	69	4	3
2	8	4	4	Typewriter	26	54	5	4

Similarly, although managers said tape recorders are readily obtainable, only 6 percent of B-TIP researchers and 12 percent of Battelle researchers use them.

A serious problem emerged: while 85 percent of Battelle managers said researchers have private offices, only 41 percent of B-TIP managers said their researchers have such privacy or potential quiet. As one B-TIP manager pointed out: "Our open offices are a major deterrent to concentration on report preparation."

How researchers write (R9)

■ Most researchers (60 percent B-TIP, 76 percent Battelle) claimed they "prepare an outline and follow it reasonably well." Then they "write, scratch, and rewrite" as they go along (33 percent B-TIP, 39 percent Battelle).

Researchers / How researchers write

Percent B-TIP	Percent Battelle	Rank B-TIP	Rank Battelle	How researchers write
60	76	1	1	Prepare an outline and follow it reasonably well
33	39	2	2	Write, scratch, and rewrite as you go along
32	25	3	4	Write a first draft quickly and then edit
28	27	4	3	Spread out all the "ingredients" of the document—e.g. figures, photos, tables, data, references — and blend together
16	10	5	6	Don't prepare an outline; just sit down and write
9	12	6	5	Hide in the library (or some other quiet place) so you won't be interrupted
4	8	7	7	Ask for help from colleagues, manager, editor
3	6	8	8	Prepare an outline, but don't follow it

■ Only 4 percent of B-TIP researchers and 8 percent of Battelle researchers said they asked for help from colleagues, managers, or editors.

■ About 11 percent average said they hid in some quiet place to avoid interruption.

One researcher explained:

> "I used to hide in the library, but got faulted for being inaccessible ...so am staying in the office now."

Another said:

> "Never sleep until the document is done!"

Help available to facilitate writing (R10, M9)

On this score, opinions differed markedly. All groups agreed that secretarial help is available to type or transcribe drafts—although many researchers claimed it is not sufficient. But look at the results on the other issues.*

Researchers				Help available to facilitate writing	**Managers**			
Percent		Rank			Percent		Rank	
B-TIP	Battelle	B-TIP	Battelle		B-TIP	Battelle	B-TIP	Battelle
72	83	1	1	Secretarial help to type written drafts or to transcribe dictated materials	82	95	1	1
41	30	2	4	Access to data bases or libraries for obtaining needed information quickly	64	59	2	5
30	44	3	2	Access to other specialists and researchers who can supply information	48	73	3	3
18	13	4	8	Reasonable time and budgets to complete writing assignments satisfactorily	44	21	4	8
17	29	5	5	Style guides, handbooks, or texts on business and technical writing	21	28	7	7
15	24	6	6	Writing courses to streamline writing methods and products	43	66	5	4
13	37	7	3	Editorial help	35	75	6	2
7	21	8	7	Designers who can convert rough concepts to finished diagrams	18	46	8	6

From the managers' view

■ **Editorial help**—Twice as many Battelle managers (75 percent) as B-TIP managers (35 percent) said that editorial help was available for researchers.

■ **Time and budgets**—On the other hand, 44 percent of B-TIP managers vs 21 percent of Battelle managers thought researchers had reasonable time and budgets to complete writing assignments satisfactorily.

■ **Writing courses**—43 percent of B-TIP managers and 66 percent of Battelle managers said they offer researchers the opportunity to attend courses to upgrade writing skills and products.

But the researchers' view is very different:

■ **Editorial help**—Only 13 percent of B-TIP researchers and 37 percent of Battelle researchers said editorial help is "available"—less than half of what managers claimed. Several Battelle researchers complained that such help was only theoretically available; actually, in view of budget constraints and high editorial costs, it was unaffordable. They viewed "art or design aid" similarly.

---

* While these data are not matched pairs from both managers and researchers at each participating facility—and thus cannot be compared directly—they do indicate trends in opinion and perception. Each responding company sent answers both from researchers and managers.

■ **Time and budgets**—Only 18 percent of B-TIP researchers and 13 percent of Battelle researchers said they had reasonable time and budgets to complete writing assignments satisfactorily.

■ **Writing courses**—Only 15 percent of B-TIP researchers and 24 percent of Battelle researchers said that writing courses were available.

The table summarizing the responses of all four groups further emphasizes these differences in viewpoint.

Guidance for researchers before starting writing tasks (R11, M10)

By far, the two main guidelines **managers** said they give researchers are:

■ **When** the document is needed (70 percent B-TIP, 81 percent Battelle)

■ **What** kind of document is needed (68 percent B-TIP, 72 percent Battelle).

Researchers				Guidance for researchers before starting writing tasks	**Managers**			
Percent		**Rank**			**Percent**		**Rank**	
B-TIP	**Battelle**	**B-TIP**	**Battelle**		**B-TIP**	**Battelle**	**B-TIP**	**Battelle**
52	45	1	2	Manager tells researcher WHAT TYPE of document is needed (e.g., report, memo, proposal)	68	72	2	2
50	49	2	1	Manager tells researcher WHEN the document is needed	70	81	1	1
32	38	3	3	Manager gives researcher NO guidance	8	3	8	8
17	14	4	4	Manager provides researcher with a GENERAL OUTLINE of the information needed in the document	38	47	3	3
13	9	5	6	Manager describes what FORMAT or ORGANIZATION the document should have	31	43	4	4
9	12	6	5	Manager specifies HOW LONG the document should be	16	31	6	5
2	5	7	7	Manager requires and reviews researchers DETAILED OUTLINE before writing starts, especially of major documents	12	30	7	6
				Manager gives the researchers' project or line managers specific guidelines for the various kinds of documents	19	23	5	7

Other guidelines are less forthcoming:

■ Fewer managers (35 percent B-TIP, 45 percent Battelle) said they give researchers a general outline or organizational guidelines (averages of **both** items).

■ 16 percent of B-TIP managers and 31 percent of Battelle managers said they tell researchers how long a document should be.

■ Fewer still (12 percent B-TIP, 30 percent Battelle) indicated they approve a detailed outline in advance.

■ About 6 percent of managers of both groups said they give researchers no guidance at all! But 19 percent of B-TIP managers and 23 percent of Battelle managers claimed they give project or line managers guidelines for various kinds of documents they need to receive.

Both B-TIP and Battelle managers ranked the kinds of guidance they give very similarly.

Researchers of both groups agreed on the prewriting guidance they get from managers. But their views differed sharply from managers' opinions:

- About 50 percent of both groups agreed that the managers told them **when and what type** documents are needed.
- But, about **35 percent (vs 6 percent of managers) claimed they received no guidance at all!**
- Only about 14 percent said they received any guidance on outlines or organization (averaged from both items).
- Only 11 percent said their managers specified **how long** documents should be.
- A mere 4 percent said their outlines were reviewed before they started writing.

These results are significant because they may reveal serious miscommunications. As one manager cautioned us, "Have you even seen what managers write to researchers?". Such results also point to some key steps for improving managers' inputs to researchers' writing.

Feedback after document is turned in (R12, M11)

You can see from the managers' results that:

- A large number of **managers** of both groups (about 65 percent) noted they comment quickly and ask for revisions.
- 65 percent of Battelle managers and 49 percent of B-TIP managers said they sometimes correct or edit a document themselves—or even completely rewrite it. (A few scratched out the phrase, "or even completely rewrite"!)
- 51 percent of Battelle and 43 percent of B-TIP managers said they take the time to explain **basic** problems and ask for **specific** improvements.
- 13 percent of Battelle and 4 percent of B-TIP managers said they gave no feedback.

Researchers				Feedback after document is turned in	Managers			
Percent		Rank			Percent		Rank	
B-TIP	Battelle	B-TIP	Battelle		B-TIP	Battelle	B-TIP	Battelle
39	45	1	1	Manager comments quickly and GENERALLY on the problems of the first draft and asks for revisions	64	66	1	1
36	40	2	2	Manager sometimes corrects or edits—or even completely rewrites—the document	49	65	2	2
18	13	3	4	None: Manager gives no feedback	4	13	5	5
16	9	4	5	Manager usually sends draft back for several rounds of revision before document is considered satisfactory	10	8	4	7
14	14	5	3	Manager sits down with researcher and explains what BASIC problems show up in the document, what SPECIFIC improvements are needed, and how such problems can be avoided in future work	43	51	3	3
1	2	6	6	Manager has an editor check researcher's document for required content and format	0	1	8	8
0	0	7	7	Manager often asks an editor to help researcher write the document	3	10	6	6
				Manager sometimes has an editor work individually with researchers on particularly tough writing problems	3	27	6	4

Again, researchers' views differed from managers' claims:

■ About 42 percent of researchers of both groups said their managers commented quickly and asked for revisions,

■ 38 percent thought their managers corrected the document.

■ But, only 14 percent said their managers actually sat down to explain what was basically wrong and to specify revisions—a sharp contrast to the average 47 percent of managers who feel they are explaining problems.

Another interesting point: all four groups agreed that editorial help is rarely used on a regular basis. However, 27 percent of Battelle managers claimed they **sometimes** used editors to work with researchers on tough writing problems, and 10 percent said they **often** used editors who understood their criteria to help researchers write better documents. These results compare to replies of 3 percent for B-TIP managers.

But, only 2 percent of researchers said that managers had an editor help them check a document for required content and format. And the percent that said the manager **often** asks an editor to help them write the document was zero! Clearly the overall use of professional editors is low.

Nine percent of managers and Battelle researchers and 16 percent of B-TIP researchers said that documents were sent back for several rounds of revision.

Value of reducing time and increasing ease of writing and reading (R13, M12)

How important would it be to reduce researchers' writing and managers' reading time, and increase ease of writing? The table best illustrates the answer.

Thus, while Battelle managers and researchers weighed in more heavily on the "extremely helpful" side, only a very small, equal percent of B-TIP and Battelle staff thought improvements in this area would not be helpful at all.

This result strongly hints that many researchers and managers are willing—even eager—to improve their writing and reading productivity.

Researchers				Value of reducing time and increasing ease of writing and reading	Managers			
Percent		Rank			Percent		Rank	
B-TIP	Battelle	B-TIP	Battelle		B-TIP	Battelle	B-TIP	Battelle
33	40	1	1	Extremely helpful	19	32	3	2
32	30	2	2	Very helpful	38	42	1	1
29	25	3	3	Somewhat helpful	37	21	2	3
3	2	4	4	Not helpful	3	2	4	4

Steps MANAGERS are willing to take to upgrade researchers' writing (M13)

Overall, B-TIP and Battelle managers agreed on the steps they are willing to take to upgrade writing:

■ Fund researchers courses based on actual assignments (52 percent average)

Steps MANAGERS are willing to take to upgrade researchers' writing	Managers			
	Percent		Rank	
	B-TIP	Battelle	B-TIP	Battelle
Provide funds for researchers to attend courses on technical/business writing, based on their actual assignments	51	52	1	2
Include improved writing skills as a positive factor in performance evaluations	49	67	2	1
Give researchers more detailed initial instructions and feedback	37	43	3	3
Encourage line managers to attend a course so they can give researchers better writing guidance	29	22	4	6
Put more time into working directly with researchers	20	27	5	5
Attend a course so you can guide researchers more effectively and easily	16	29	6	4
Provide researchers with more equipment and help (e.g., tape recorders, secretarial help, computer terminals) to facilitate their writing tasks	16	19	6	8
Employ a technical editor to review incoming documents and help researchers individually as needed	9	20	8	7

■ Include improved writing skills as a positive factor in performance evaluations (49 percent B-TIP; 67 percent Battelle)

■ Give researchers more detailed guidance and feedback (37 percent B-TIP; 43 percent Battelle).

Furthermore, some interest was shown (about 29 percent B-TIP, 22 percent Battelle) in encouraging line managers to attend a course on giving researchers better guidance. Some managers were willing to attend such a course themselves (16 percent B-TIP, 29 percent Battelle).

However, only 16 percent of B-TIP and 19 percent of Battelle managers were ready to furnish better equipment—e.g., PCs, tape recorders, or more secretarial help. More Battelle managers than B-TIP managers (20 vs 9 percent) expressed willingness to employ technical editors to review incoming documents and to assist researchers as needed.

Actions researchers would find helpful to improve their writing (R14)

By contrast, the two actions that researchers singled out to help them improve their writing were:

■ Have their own terminal and wordprocessing software so they can write and make revisions easily by themselves (27 percent B-TIP; 36 percent Battelle)

■ Have more time to do a better writing job (26 percent B-TIP; 37 percent Battelle).

However, three other actions received some researchers' support:

■ Receive clear and specific feedback from managers (22 percent B-TIP, 18 percent Battelle)

■ Work with an experienced editor who can help pinpoint and resolve individual writing difficulties (21 percent B-TIP, 24 percent Battelle)

■ Attend a course on scientific/business writing based on actual writing tasks (20 percent B-TIP, 17 percent Battelle).

Researchers

Percent		Rank		Actions researchers would find helpful to improve their writing
B-TIP	Battelle	B-TIP	Battelle	
27	36	1	2	Have your own terminal and wordprocessing software to write and revise more easily yourself
26	37	2	1	Have more time to do a better writing job
22	18	3	4	Receive clear and specific feedback from your manager
21	24	4	3	Work with an experienced editor who can help you pinpoint and resolve your writing difficulties
20	17	5	5	Attend a course on scientific/business writing, based on your actual writing tasks
13	7	6	7	Receive more detailed instructions or outlines from your manager
11	10	7	6	Have better equipment and help (e.g., secretarial help, tape recorder) to facilitate writing
6	7	8	7	Have your manager approve your outline BEFORE you start writing

Again, these results point to key areas where investments in improvement are likely to be effective. Note, however, that all the percentages are on the low side. Could it be that many researchers are resigned to "crash" writing tasks? to relatively little chance for meaningful help?

Ratings for writing (M14, and final personal history question on both questionnaires—not shown here)

Instructive tables that demonstrate the complexity of the technical/business writing problem show the answers to 3 questions:

■ To managers, "Overall, on a scale of 1 to 5 (1 is poor, 5 is excellent) how would you rate the quality of researchers' writing?"

■ To researchers "How do you rate yourself as a writer of technical/business documents?"

■ To managers, "How do you rate yourself as a writer?".

How managers rated researchers
Percent response

SCALE Respondents	1	2	3	4	5
B-TIP managers	0	22	58	15	0
Battelle managers	0	16	67	14	0

How researchers rated themselves
Percent response

	1	2	3	4	5
B-TIP researchers	1	10	39	38	4
Battelle researchers	0	3	35	45	10

How managers rated themselves
Percent response

	1	2	3	4	5
B-TIP managers	0	2	26	55	6
Battelle managers	0	0	21	65	8

At first glance, this result seems to indicate a vast difference in perception of the quality of researchers' writing: a total of 42 percent of B-TIP researchers and 55 percent of Battelle researchers rated themselves as 4 or 5 on the scale, whereas both groups of managers rated only 15 percent (average) of researchers as 4's, and none as 5's! However, we need to remember that managers gave an average rating to researchers as a group, while researchers and managers rated themselves individually.

Notice that managers as a whole rated themselves higher than researchers rated themselves. Personal history data showed that about 95 percent of the managers of both groups had worked previously as researchers; about 75 percent of them had worked as researchers for 6 years or more. This result may support conjectures that good writing skills are a prerequisite for advancement.*

Still, numerous managers hesitated to give an average rating of 3 without adding caveats such as:

> "New graduates probably get a 1.0 rating."
> "Great variation from individual to individual."
> "Range is 1 to 5; mostly in 2 to 3 range."
> "They range from 2 to 4."

One manager put it this way:

> "3—worse than newspaper reporters; better than agency
> copywriters or bureaucrats."

Steps managers are willing to take to help RESEARCHERS upgrade writing quality (M15)

■ By far, the largest percentage of managers (51 percent B-TIP; 61 percent Battelle) were willing to send researchers to 20 to 40 hour in-house writing courses based on researchers' actual work and specific writing needs.

Steps managers are willing to take to help RESEARCHERS upgrade writing	Managers			
	Percent		Rank	
	B-TIP	Battelle	B-TIP	Battelle
Send researchers to a 20- to 40-hour in-house writing course based on their actual work, and designed specifically to address their writing needs	51	61	1	1
Give researchers 1 hour weekly for 10 weeks to work with an instructor	27	33	2	3
Allot researchers time to prepare for courses and to practice what they learn	27	13	2	5
Allow researchers 20 hours over a period of 3 to 6 months to receive individual instruction	22	38	4	2
Send researchers to off-site writing courses for 20 to 40 hours	19	23	5	4
Fund the development and implementation of such a course (i.e., based on researchers' actual work)	13	13	6	5

* In an MIT study, the authors observed that "writing...ability may be one of the factors in the selection process that moves people into higher administrative roles". See reference 1.

■ Fewer were willing to support individual instruction (27 percent B-TIP; 33 percent Battelle).

■ Off-site courses were favored by a still smaller group (19 percent B-TIP; 23 percent Battelle).

■ B-TIP managers were more willing than Battelle managers (27 vs 13 percent) to allot researchers time to prepare for courses and to practice what they learn.

Instruction managers have already made available (M16)

Instruction managers have already made available	Managers			
	Percent		Rank	
	B-TIP	Battelle	B-TIP	Battelle
In-house courses to improve writing skills	55	83	1	1
Short business communications courses	20	9	2	4
University courses in technical writing	12	10	3	3
Individual instruction in-house from editors or consultants	10	26	4	2

■ 55 percent of B-TIP managers and a whopping 83 percent of Battelle managers stated that in-house courses to improve writing skills have already been made available to researchers.*

■ Although more B-TIP managers than Battelle managers (20 vs 9 percent) said that short courses in business communications were available, more Battelle managers (26 vs 10 percent) said individual instruction was available from in-house editors or consultants.

■ Only a small percent of managers of both groups (average 11 percent) said that they had made university courses in technical writing available.

Instruction researchers have received

Though managers overwhelmingly claimed courses are available,

■ Only about 34 percent of both groups of researchers said they had taken in-house courses.

Researchers				Instruction researchers have received
Percent		Rank		
B-TIP	Battelle	B-TIP	Battelle	
32	37	1	1	In-house courses to improve writing skills
31	36	2	2	University courses in business writing
10	9	3	4	Short courses in business communications
6	15	4	3	Individual instruction from in-house editors or from consultants

* Note that these percentages are higher than those for similar items in question M9, R10 and in M15. This difference suggests that, while courses may be available, researchers may not always have the opportunity to attend.

■ An average of 33 percent said they had taken university courses in technical writing.

■ But only 6 percent of B-TIP researchers and 15 percent of Battelle researchers said they had received individual instruction from in-house editors or consultants.

Effects of instruction on writing abilities (R16, M17)

How effective have these courses been?

The opinions of **researchers** who had taken writing courses are shown in the table. Battelle researchers seem to have benefited more than their B-TIP colleagues in the top two areas, writing organization and clarity. Overall, however, these results suggest that such courses, at least as presently constructed, do not yield an adequate "return on investment".

Researchers

Percent		Rank		Effects of instruction on writing abilities
B-TIP	**Battelle**	**B-TIP**	**Battelle**	
27	43	1	1	You organize writing projects better
25	32	2	2	You write more clearly
22	21	3	3	You write more concisely
18	18	4	5	Your writing skills improved slightly
17	20	5	4	You try to include relevant information only
7	12	6	6	You write more quickly
7	5	6	7	Helped you at first; but improvement wore off
4	2	8	8	The instruction did not help you at all

Managers' observations on the effects of such courses further reinforce this conclusion.

	Managers			
Effects of instruction on researchers' writing	Percent		Rank	
	B-TIP	**Battelle**	**B-TIP**	**Battelle**
Minor improvements could be observed	37	41	1	1
Their writing became much easier to understand	12	10	2	4
Documents became shorter and more relevant to business needs	11	11	3	3
Lasting improvements took place	8	18	4	2
No improvement was evident	8	7	4	6
Major improvements occurred, but were short term	7	9	6	5
Documents could be read more quickly	5	7	7	6

Clearly, these results indicate that we need to reexamine the content and structure of writing courses, and their relation to actual work. We also need to reevaluate our expectations for improvements in writing skills.

QUESTIONNAIRE

"Helping Researchers Write... So Managers Can Understand"

Part 1: Questions for managers

Instructions

■ You can check off more than one response to each question . . .

■ But please select your MAIN responses only.

■ Please use the "OTHER" line at the end of each question to add your comments and suggestions or to qualify your responses. REMEMBER: The answers listed here are general; and they are not comprehensive. But we hope they will trigger more specific replies based on your experience.

---

1. **What main types of researchers' writing do you need to read or review?**

   ☐ proposals

   ☐ memos

   ☐ reports on research projects

   ☐ requests for funding new product or new technology development

   ☐ technical evaluations of proposed R&D

   ☐ technology development and budget plans of R&D groups

   ☐ technical articles for scientific journals or conferences

   ☐ technical communications for non-specialists (e.g., for company staff, shareholders, or the general public)

   ☐ OTHER types of writing _____

   _____

   _____

2. **What percent of your total working time is spent reading this technical/business material?**

   ☐ 0 to 20%

   ☐ 21 to 40%

   ☐ 41 to 60%

   ☐ 61 to 80%

   ☐ 81 to 100%

3. **What key writing qualities do you look for in researchers' technical/business documents?**

   ☐ clear, unambiguous writing

   ☐ conciseness

   ☐ easily read and understood technical explanations

   ☐ useful information on the business impacts of the technology

   ☐ easily grasped, logical organization

   ☐ relevant, accurate information in response to requests

   ☐ compliance with requested format

   ☐ good grammar and almost-error-free spelling

   ☐ OTHER key qualities you want _____

   _____

4. **Are researchers' written communications important in your company because they are used to help**

   ☐ decide on R&D directions and investments

   ☐ stimulate and synergize new ideas

   ☐ identify and evaluate new product concepts

   ☐ obtain clients for contract research

   ☐ boost R&D productivity

   ☐ communicate R&D results throughout the company

   ☐ prevent decisions based on vague or undocumented information

   ☐ advance researchers' careers

   ☐ OTHER reasons _____

   _____

PLEASE pay special attention to the next three questions: they try to pinpoint the difficulties with researchers' writing that you encounter most often. Please write your comments, caveats, or suggestions on the ''OTHER'' line at the end of the question. (If you need more room, use the space on page 4 of this questionnaire—or attach another sheet of paper.)

To help you answer, these questions are loosely grouped as problems in CONTENT, MECHANICS, and STYLE. But in fact these areas are closely interrelated.

5. **What are the main problems you face in the CONTENT of researchers' writing?**
   - ☐ the impacts of technological advances on the company's business needs, problems, and goals are inadequately addressed
   - ☐ too much technical detail
   - ☐ explanations of general technological concepts are unclear
   - ☐ extraneous and irrelevant material included; not responsive to requests for information
   - ☐ poor or cumbersome organization
   - ☐ information is difficult to scan and grasp quickly
   - ☐ logic leading to conclusions is unclear, unconvincing, or lacking
   - ☐ conclusions and recommendations not spelled out in business terms
   - ☐ OTHER problems in CONTENT _____

   _____

6. **What are the main problems you find in the MECHANICS of researchers' writing?**
   - ☐ faulty grammar
   - ☐ poor sentence construction (e.g., sentences are too long, awkward, or similar in form)
   - ☐ spelling errors
   - ☐ imprecise word choice
   - ☐ too much jargon; many undefined technical terms
   - ☐ improper punctuation
   - ☐ OTHER problems in MECHANICS of writing

   _____

7. **What are the main problems you find in the STYLE of researchers' writing?**
   - ☐ cluttered; overly elaborate
   - ☐ too long; not concise
   - ☐ hard to read and understand; focus and meaning unclear
   - ☐ poor transitions; writing leaps from one point to another
   - ☐ requested format not followed
   - ☐ variation in quality of writing from the SAME researcher
   - ☐ great variation of input from DIFFERENT researchers
   - ☐ not persuasive
   - ☐ OTHER problems in STYLE _____

   _____

8. **What equipment and surroundings do you make available to help researchers write?**
   - ☐ pen and paper
   - ☐ typewriter
   - ☐ tape recorder
   - ☐ personal computer or word processing terminal
   - ☐ private, quiet office
   - ☐ OTHER equipment _____

   _____

   _____

   _____

9. **What help do you offer researchers to facilitate their writing tasks?**
   - ☐ secretarial help to type written drafts or to transcribe dictated material
   - ☐ editorial help
   - ☐ access to data bases or libraries
   - ☐ access to other specialists and researchers
   - ☐ design assistance to convert rough concepts to finished diagrams
   - ☐ courses to upgrade writing skills and products
   - ☐ style guides (either company or outside), handbooks, or texts on business and technical writing
   - ☐ reasonable time and budgets to complete writing assignments satisfactorily
   - ☐ OTHER help to facilitate writing _____

   _____

   _____

   _____

10. **How much guidance do you give researchers before they start a writing task? (For this question, check off ALL the answers that apply to you.)**
    - ☐ none
    - ☐ I tell researchers WHAT TYPE of document is needed
    - ☐ I tell them WHEN the document is needed
    - ☐ I specify HOW LONG the document should be
    - ☐ I describe the FORMAT or ORGANIZATION the document should have
    - ☐ I give them a general OUTLINE of the information needed
    - ☐ I review and approve their DETAILED OUTLINES before they start writing—especially for long, major documents
    - ☐ I give the researchers' project or line managers specific guidelines for the various kinds of documents I need to receive
    - ☐ OTHER writing guidance _____

    _____

    _____

11. **What feedback do you give researchers after you receive their written document? (Again, check all answers that apply to you.)**

☐ none

☐ I sometimes correct or edit—or even completely rewrite—the document myself

☐ I comment quickly and generally on the problems of the first draft and ask for revisions

☐ I take the time to sit down with researchers, explain what BASIC problems show up in their document, what SPECIFIC improvements are needed, and how these problems can be avoided

☐ I usually have to send the draft back for several rounds of revisions until the document is satisfactory

☐ I OFTEN use an editor who understands my criteria to help researchers write better documents

☐ I SOMETIMES have an editor work individually with researchers on particularly tough writing problems

☐ I have an editor work with researchers' managers to assure production of documents with the content and format needed for making business decisions

☐ OTHER feedback _____

_____

12. **How helpful would it be if you could reduce the amount of time you spend reading and critiquing researchers' technical/business writing, and increase the ease with which you understand this material?**

☐ extremely helpful

☐ very helpful

☐ somewhat helpful

☐ not helpful

☐ OTHER comments _____

13. **What steps would YOU be willing to take to upgrade the quality of researchers' writing?**

☐ put more time into working directly with researchers

☐ attend a course so you can guide researchers more effectively and easily

☐ encourage line managers to attend a course so they can give researchers better writing guidance

☐ give researchers more detailed initial instructions and feedback

☐ provide researchers with more equipment and help (e.g., tape recorders, secretarial help, computer terminals) to facilitate their writing tasks

☐ employ a technical editor to review incoming documents and to assist researchers individually as needed

☐ provide funds for researchers to attend courses on business/technical writing, based on their actual assignments

☐ include improved writing skills as a positive factor in performance evaluations

☐ OTHER steps _____

_____

14. **Overall, on a scale of 1 to 5 (1 is poor, 5 is excellent) how would you rate the quality of researchers' writing?**

_____

☐ OTHER comments and caveats _____

_____

_____

_____

15. **What steps would you be willing to take to help RESEARCHERS upgrade the quality of their writing?**

☐ send them to off-site writing courses for 20 to 40 hours

☐ send them to a 20-to-40-hour in-house writing course based on their actual work, and designed specifically to address their writing needs

☐ fund the development and implementation of such a course

☐ give them 1 hour weekly for 10 weeks to work with an instructor

☐ allow them 20 hours over a period of 3 to 6 months to receive individual instruction

☐ allot them time to prepare for courses and to practice what they learn

☐ OTHER steps _____

_____

16. **What instruction have you already made available to researchers?**

☐ university courses in technical writing

☐ short courses in business communications

☐ in-house courses to improve writing skills

☐ individual instruction in-house from editors or consultants

☐ OTHER types of instruction _____

_____

17. **If you checked any of the items in Question 16, what effects did this instruction have on researchers' writing?**

☐ their writing became much easier to understand

☐ documents could be read more quickly

☐ documents became shorter and more relevant to business needs

☐ lasting improvements took place

☐ major improvements occurred, but were short term

☐ minor improvements could be observed

☐ no improvement was evident

☐ OTHER effects of instruction _____

_____

QUESTIONNAIRE

"Helping Researchers Write... So Managers Can Understand"

Part 2: Questions for researchers

Instructions

■ You can check off more than one response to each question . . .

■ But please select only your MAIN responses.

■ Please use the "OTHER" line at the end of each question to add your comments and suggestions or to qualify your responses. REMEMBER: The answers listed here are general; and they are not comprehensive. But we hope they will trigger more specific replies based on your experience.

---

1. **What main types of documents do you need to write?**
   - ☐ proposals
   - ☐ reports on research projects
   - ☐ memos
   - ☐ requests for funding new product or new technology development
   - ☐ technical evaluations of proposed R&D investments
   - ☐ plans and budgets for technology development in your R&D group
   - ☐ technical articles for scientific journals or conferences
   - ☐ technical communications for non-specialists (e.g., for company staff, shareholders, or the general public)
   - ☐ OTHER types of writing _____
   - _____
   - _____

2. **What percent of your total work time is spent writing?**
   - ☐ 0 to 20%
   - ☐ 21 to 40%
   - ☐ 41 to 60%
   - ☐ 61 to 80%
   - ☐ 81 to 100%

3. **What key qualities do you think the technical/business material you write for managers and executives should have?**
   - ☐ clear, unambiguous writing
   - ☐ conciseness
   - ☐ easily read and understood technical explanations
   - ☐ useful information on the business impacts of the technology you're dealing with
   - ☐ easily grasped, logical organization
   - ☐ relevant, accurate information in response to requests
   - ☐ required format
   - ☐ correct grammar and almost-error-free spelling
   - ☐ OTHER key qualities of technical/business documents _____
   - _____

4. **Are researchers' written communications important in your company because they are used to help**
   - ☐ decide on R&D directions and investments
   - ☐ stimulate and synergize new ideas
   - ☐ identify and evaluate, new product concepts
   - ☐ obtain clients for contract research
   - ☐ boost R&D productivity
   - ☐ communicate R&D results throughout the company
   - ☐ prevent decisions based on vague or undocumented information
   - ☐ advance researchers' careers
   - ☐ OTHER reasons _____
   - _____

PLEASE pay special attention to the next three questions: they try to pinpoint the main writing difficulties you have. And please write your comments, caveats, or suggestions on the "OTHER" line at the end of each question. (If you need more room, use the space on page 4 of this questionnaire—or attach another sheet of paper.)

To help you answer, these questions are loosely grouped as problems in CONTENT, MECHANICS, and PROCEDURES. But in fact these areas are closely interrelated.

5. What are the main CONTENT problems you face in writing?
- ☐ figuring out what the manager or the information requester really wants to know
- ☐ deciding what technical information and level of detail to include
- ☐ simplifying the descriptions of technical problems and technological concepts for the non-specialist manager
- ☐ developing and including the requested business information
- ☐ organizing the document to facilitate reading and grasp
- ☐ writing the transitions from one point to another
- ☐ making sure the logic leading to your conclusions is clear and convincing, and doesn't have gaps
- ☐ OTHER problems in CONTENT _____

_____

6. What are your main problems in the MECHANICS of writing?
- ☐ choosing the exact words
- ☐ avoiding jargon
- ☐ spelling
- ☐ structuring sentences so they are easy to read
- ☐ using correct grammar
- ☐ punctuating correctly
- ☐ producing documents of the prescribed length
- ☐ following requested formats
- ☐ OTHER problems in MECHANICS _____

_____

7. What are your main problems in the PROCEDURES of writing?
- ☐ getting started
- ☐ preparing a useful outline or plan
- ☐ sticking to the outline
- ☐ writing the first draft
- ☐ revising and editing your own draft
- ☐ finding large enough chunks of time to write efficiently
- ☐ meeting short, frequent deadlines
- ☐ producing quality writing within allotted budgets
- ☐ OTHER problems in PROCEDURES _____

_____

8. What tools do you use when you write?
- ☐ pencil and paper
- ☐ tape recorder
- ☐ typewriter
- ☐ computer with word processing
- ☐ OTHER tools _____

_____

_____

9. How do you go about your writing tasks?
- ☐ prepare an outline and follow it reasonably well
- ☐ prepare an outline, but don't follow it
- ☐ don't prepare an outline; just sit down and write
- ☐ spread out all the "ingredients" of the document —e.g., figures, photos, tables, data, references— and blend together
- ☐ write a first draft quickly, and then edit
- ☐ write, scratch, and rewrite as you go along
- ☐ ask for help from colleagues, manager, editor
- ☐ hide in the library (or some other quiet place) so you won't be interrupted
- ☐ OTHER ways you go about writing _____

_____

_____

10. What help is available to make your writing task easier?
- ☐ secretarial help to type written drafts or to transcribe dictated materials
- ☐ editorial help
- ☐ data bases or libraries for obtaining needed information quickly
- ☐ other specialists and researchers who can supply information
- ☐ designers who can convert rough concepts to finished diagrams
- ☐ writing courses to streamline your writing methods and products
- ☐ style guides, handbooks, or texts on business and technical writing
- ☐ reasonable time and budgets to complete writing assignments satisfactorily
- ☐ OTHER _____

_____

_____

Helping researchers write...

11. **How much guidance does your manager give you BEFORE you start a writing task? (For this question, check ALL answers that apply to you.)**
   ☐ none
   ☐ manager tells you WHAT TYPE of document is needed (e.g., report, memo, proposal)
   ☐ . . . tells you WHEN the document is needed
   ☐ . . . specifies HOW LONG the document should be
   ☐ . . . describes what FORMAT or ORGANIZATION the document should have
   ☐ . . . provides a GENERAL OUTLINE of the information needed in the document
   ☐ . . . requires and reviews your DETAILED OUTLINE before you start writing—especially for long, major documents
   ☐ OTHER writing guidance _____
   _____
   _____

12. **What feedback does your manager give you AFTER you turn in a document? (Again, check ALL answers that apply.)**
   ☐ none
   ☐ manager sometimes corrects or edits—or even completely rewrites—the document
   ☐ . . . comments quickly and generally on the problems of the first draft and asks for revisions
   ☐ . . . sits down with you and explains what BASIC problems show up in the document, what SPECIFIC improvements are needed, and how such problems can be avoided in future work
   ☐ . . . usually sends draft back for several rounds of revision before the document is considered satisfactory
   ☐ . . . often asks an editor to help you write the document
   ☐ . . . has an editor check the document for required content and format
   ☐ OTHER feedback _____
   _____
   _____

13. **How helpful would it be if you could reduce your writing time and increase your ease of writing?**
   ☐ extremely helpful
   ☐ very helpful
   ☐ somewhat helpful
   ☐ not helpful
   ☐ OTHER _____
   _____

14. **What actions would help you most to improve your writing?**
   ☐ receive more detailed instructions or outlines from your manager
   ☐ have your manager approve your outline BEFORE you start writing
   ☐ receive clear and specific feedback from your manager
   ☐ have better equipment and help (e.g., secretarial help, tape recorder) to facilitate writing
   ☐ have your own terminal and wordprocessing software so you can write and make revisions more easily yourself
   ☐ attend a course on scientific/business writing, based on your actual writing tasks
   ☐ work with an experienced editor who can help you pinpoint and resolve your writing difficulties
   ☐ have more time to do a better writing job
   ☐ OTHER helpful actions _____
   _____
   _____

15. **What writing instruction have you already received?**
   ☐ university courses on technical writing
   ☐ short courses on business communications
   ☐ in-house courses to improve writing skills
   ☐ individual instruction from in-house editors or from consultants
   ☐ OTHER types of instruction _____
   _____
   _____

16. **If you checked any of the items in question 15, how have these courses affected your writing abilities?**
   ☐ you write more quickly
   ☐ you write more clearly
   ☐ you organize writing projects better
   ☐ you write more concisely
   ☐ you try to include relevant information only
   ☐ helped you at first; but improvement wore off
   ☐ your writing skills improved slightly
   ☐ the instruction did not help you at all
   ☐ OTHER results of writing courses _____
   _____

REFERENCES

1. J. Paradis, D. Dobrin, and R. Miller, "Writing at Exxon ITD: Notes on the Writing Environment of an R&D Organization", from *Writing in Non-Academic Settings,* Eds. L. Odell and D. Goswami, Guilford Press, New York, 1985, pp. 281-307. We highly recommend reading this insightful article.

2. J.J. Duga and W.H. Fisher, *Probable Levels of R&D Expenditures in 1993: Forecast and Analysis,* Battelle-Columbus, 1992

3. *The ACS Style Guide, A Manual for Authors and Editors,* J.E. Dodd, Editor, American Chemical Society, Washington, D.C., 1986.

4. B-TIP Review No. 5[*], *Idea Generation Methods: Creative Solutions to Business and Technical Problems,* Battelle Memorial Institute, Columbus, Ohio, 1981.

5. D. Landreman, "A New look at Outlining—the LSN-SN Approach", *Proceedings, 21st International Technical Communications Conference,* May 1974, St. Louis, Missouri. Ms. Landreman, a former senior proposal writer at Battelle, taught this technique for many years in an in-house writing course.

6. R.C. Wydick, *Plain English for Lawyers,* 2nd edition, Carolina Academic Press, Durham, North Carolina, 1985.

7. B-TIP Review No. 21[*], *Rapid Solidification: Updating the "New Metallurgy",* Battelle Memorial Institute, Columbus, Ohio, 1985.

8. B-TIP Report No. 46[*], *Bioseparations Technology: Problems and Prospects,* Battelle Memorial Institute, Columbus, Ohio, 1985.

9. Personal communication from A. Sageev, then Assistant Professor, Department of Petroleum Engineering, Stanford University, July 1985.

10. Personal communication from J. Paradis, Associate Professor, Writing Program, Massachusetts Institute of Technology, March 1986.

11. "Computer-aided Innovative Thinking", B-TIP *Technology Sensor,* No. 39[*], Battelle Memorial Institute, Columbus, Ohio, April 1986.

12. B-TIP Review No. 23[*], *Group Dynamic Methods for Forecasting and Strategic Planning,* Battelle Memorial Institute, Columbus, Ohio, 1986.

13. Personal communication with R.O. Barclay, April and June, 1994. See also R.O. Barclay, T.E. Pinelli, D. Elazar, and J. M. Kennedy, "An analysis of the Technical Communication Practices Reported by Israeli and U.S. Aerospace Engineers and Scientists", *Proceedings of "The Engineered Communication": Conference of the International Professional Communications Section of the IEEE,* Vol. II, published by the IEEE (Institute of Electrical and Electronic Engineers), Oct. 1991. This article presents the results of part of a wide ranging research project these and other authors are conducting on this topic. Their work covers aerospace engineers in, for example, Holland, Germany, Japan, Russia, Israel, and other countries. For other articles on this subject, see: Thomas E. Pinelli; Rebecca O. Barclay; Michael L. Keene; Madelyn Flammia; and John M. Kennedy, "The Technical Communication Practices of Russian and U.S. Aerospace Engineers and Scientists". *IEEE Transactions on Professional Communication,* Volume 36, No. 2 (June 1993): 95–104. Also, Rebecca O. Barclay; et al, "The Technical Communications Practices of Dutch and U.S. Aerospace Engineers and Scientists: International Perspectives on Aerospace". *IEEE Transactions on Professional Communication,* Volume 37, No. 2 (July 1994).

14. J.B. Bennett, *Editing for Engineers,* Wiley-Interscience, Division of John Wiley & Sons, New York, 1970. This book describes the manager's role as an editor and a writing coach.

15. Personal communication with Dr. Susan Dressel, Staff to the Director of Computation, Information, and Communication Division, Los Alamos National Laboratories, Los Alamos, NM, October 1992, January 1994.

16. Personal communications with Prof. Jan H. Spyridakis, Department of Technical Communications, School of Engineering, University of Washington, Seattle, WA, 1987, 1991,1992, and 1994.

17. R.D. Gieselman, "Megatrends: The Future of Business Writing, Technical Writing, and Composition", *Bulletin of the Association for Business Communication,* Vol. XLVIII, No. 4, Dec. 1985.

18. L.W. Denton, "In-House Training in Written Communication: A Status Report", *The Journal of Business Communication,* Vol. 16, No. 3, Spring 1979.

BIBLIOGRAPHY

Chicago Manual of Style, 13th edition, University of Chicago Press, Chicago, Illinois, 1982.

L.S. King, M.D., *"Why Not Say It Clearly: A Guide to Scientific Writing",* Little Brown and Company, Boston, 1978. A useful book by the former Senior Editor of the Journal of the American Medical Association.

J.C. Mathes and D.W. Stenson, *Designing Technical Reports,* The Bobbs-Merrill Company, Inc., Indianapolis, 1976. This book offers a detailed procedure for audience analysis as a first step in writing technical reports.

E. Mazzatenta, "Why Scientists Don't Write Up to Their Capabilities, or The Case of the Cringing Communicator", *Etcetera,* Vol. 38, No. 2, Summer 1981.

R.R. Rathbone, *Communicating Technical Information,* Addison-Wesley Publishing Co., Inc., Reading, MA, 1985.

J. Souther and M. White, *Technical Report Writing,* 2nd edition, Wiley, New York, 1977.

W. Strunk Jr. and B. White, *Elements of Style,* 3rd edition, Macmillan Publishing Co. Inc., New York, 1979.

Words Into Type, based on studies by M.E. Skellen, R.M Gay, and other authorities, 3rd edition, Prentice Hall, Inc., Englewood Cliffs, New Jersey, 1974.

---

[*] Contact the B-TIP office about receiving copies of these reports.